D0977540

EVERY PERSON'S
GUIDE TO
JEWISH PHILOSOPHY
AND PHILOSOPHERS

EVERY PERSON'S GUIDE TO JEWISH PHILOSOPHY AND PHILOSOPHERS

RONALD H. ISAACS

JASON ARONSON INC.
Northvale, New Jersey
Jerusalem

This book was set in 11 pt. ITC Garamond Light by Alabama Book Composition of Deatsville, AL and printed and bound by Book-mart Press, Inc. of North Bergen, NJ.

Library of Congress Cataloging-in-Publication Data

Isaacs, Ronald H.
    Every person's guide to Jewish philosophy and philosophers /
  by Ronald H. Isaacs.
        p. cm.
    Includes bibliographical references and index.
    ISBN 0-7657-6017-7
    1. Philosophy, Jewish—History. 2. Jewish philosophers—
  Biography. I. Title.
  B154.I73   1998
  181'.06—dc21   98-5334

Printed in the United States of America. Jason Aronson Inc. offers books and cassettes. For information and catalog write to Jason Aronson Inc., 230 Livingston Street, Northvale, NJ 07647-1726, or visit our website: http://www.aronson.com

In memory of
Joshua Weinstein,
my beloved father-in-law
and Professor of Philosophy

CONTENTS

Preface   xix

INTRODUCTION TO JEWISH PHILOSOPHY   1
Biblical and Rabbinic Antecedents   2
Rabbinic Literature   4

SPIRITUAL MONOTHEISM AND PHILO JUDAEUS   7
The Beginning of Jewish Philosophy   7
Philo Judaeus: The Father of Medieval Philosophy   9
God's Existence   10
God's Essence   10
God's Name   11
God's Oneness   11
God's Communication with People   12
God's Relation to the Word—Philo's Logos   12
The Problem of Evil   13
Man as a Moral Being   14
In Summation   15

MEDIEVAL JEWISH PHILOSOPHY   17
Mutazilite Kalam   18
Neoplatonism   18
Aristotelianism   19
Critics of Aristotelianism   19

SAADIA GAON: THE FIRST PHILOSOPHER OF THE MIDDLE AGES   21
Background   21
Saadia the Halakhist   22
Philosophy   23
Theory of the World   23
Nature of God   24
Mitzvot   25
The Nature of Man   25
Saadia as Liturgist   26
In Summation   26

NEOPLATONISM: SOLOMON IBN GABIROL   27
Background   27
Philosophy   28
Ethics   29
Poetry   30
In Summation   31

BACHYA IBN PAKUDA   33
Background   33
Duties of the Heart   33
Man's Soul and the Commandments   35
Worship of the Divine   35
In Summation   36

JUDAH HALEVI: POET-PHILOSOPHER EXTRAORDINAIRE   37
Background   37
The Kuzari   38
Prophecy   40

Criticism of Christianity and Islam 40
Halevi's Concept of "Divine Influence" 41
Halevi's Poems 41
In Summation 42

ARISTOTELIANISM: ABRAHAM BEN DAVID
HALEVI IBN DAUD 43
Background 43
Philosophy 44
God 44
The Soul, Prophecy and Free Will 45
In Summation 46

THE NEO-ARISTOTELIANISM OF MOSES MAIMONIDES 47
The Man and His Culture 47
God in Maimonides' Principles of Faith 49
Proofs of the Existence of God 54
Maimonides' Negative Theology 55
Origin of Evil 56
Purpose of the Divine Commandments 56
Educational Philosophy 57
In Summation 59

MOSES BEN NACHMAN (NACHMONIDES) 61
Background 61
Biblical Commentary and Philosophy 62
Nachmonides as Halakhist 63
In Summation 64

LEVI BEN GERSHOM 67
Background 67
Biblical Commentaries 67
Philosophy 68
God's Omniscience 68

God's Providence   70
Creation of the World and Miracles   70
Eschatology   72
In Summation   72

CRITICS OF ARISTOTELIANISM: HASDAI CRESCAS   73
Background   73
Or Adonai   74
Philosophy   76
God, Soul, and the Messiah   76
In Summation   77

JOSEPH ALBO   80
Background   80
Book of Principles   80
Albo's Concept of Divine Law   81
In Summation   82

ISAAC ABRABANEL   83
Background   83
Abrabanel as Author and Commentator   84
Abrabanel as Critical Biblical Interpreter   84
Abrabanel as Philosopher   85
Abrabanel as Apologete   86
Abrabanel's Understanding of History   87
Eschatology   88
In Summation   88

MYSTICISM AND ISAAC LURIA   91
Background   91
Luria's Kabbalistic God   93
Luria's Three Stages of Creation   94
Luria's Five Souls   96
In Summation   97

PANTHEISM AND BARUCH SPINOZA 99
Background 99
Spinoza's Philosophy 100
God's Nature 100
Body and Mind 102
Knowledge 102
Man's Freedom 102
Political Theory 103
Spinoza as Bible Commentator 104
In Summation 104

MOSES MENDELSSOHN 107
Background 107
Philosophy of Religion 108
God's Existence 109
Immortality of the Soul 109
Man's Freedom of Choice 110
Civil Rights 110
Mendelssohn on Judaism 111
Attitude toward Christianity 111
In Summation 112

SAMUEL DAVID LUZZATTO 113
Background 113
Attitudes toward Judaism 114
Philosophy 115
In Summation 116

NEO-ORTHODOXY AND SAMSON RAPHAEL HIRSCH 117
Background 117
Attitude toward Reform 118
Jewish Education 119
Hirsch's Conception of Judaism 119
Hirsch's View of the Commandments 120
Bible Translation 121

The Jewish People 121
In Summation 122

REFORM JUDAISM AND ABRAHAM GEIGER 123
Background 123
Philosophy 124
Geiger's Writings 125
In Summation 125

ISRAEL SALANTER 127
Background 127
Ethical Ideas 128
In Summation 129

ZECHARIAH FRANKEL 131
Background 131
Religious Outlook 131
Writings 132
In Summation 133

THE NEO-KANTIANISM OF HERMANN COHEN 135
Background 135
Cohen's Philosophic System 136
Ethics and the Idea of God 136
Cohen's Revolutionary New God Idea 137
Correlation between God and Man 138
God's Commandments 138
In Summation 139

SOLOMON SCHECHTER 141
Background 141
Catholic Israel 142
Theology 143
Sin as Rebellion 143
In Summation 144

ABRAHAM ISAAC KOOK	145
Background	145
Kook's Mysticism	146
Social Philosophy	146
Current Challenges to Religion	147
The Jews as Chosen People	147
In Summation	148
LEO BAECK	149
Background	149
Nature of God	150
Mysteries and Commandments	150
Essence of Judaism	151
Good and Evil	151
Christianity and Zionism	152
In Summation	152
FRANZ ROSENZWEIG	153
Background	153
Star of Redemption	155
Book 1: Man, the Universe, and God	155
Book 2: Revelation of God	155
Book 3: Search for the Kingdom of God	156
In Summation	157
MARTIN BUBER AND HIS DIALOGICAL PHILOSOPHY	159
The Man and His Culture	159
Hasidut	160
Haskalah	162
Secular Intellectualism	163
I and Thou	164
Between Man and Nature	166
Between Man and Man	166
God, the Eternal Thou	167
Buber and Evil	168

Buber and Humanistic Education 168
In Summation 170

MORDECAI KAPLAN: JUDAISM AS A CIVILIZATION 171
Background 171
Judaism as a Civilization 172
Kaplan's Naturalism 173
Implications of Kaplan's Theology 174
In Summation 175

MILTON STEINBERG 177
Background 177
God and Faith 178
Evil 178
Prayer 179
Jewish Religion 179
In Summation 180

MENACHEM MENDEL SCHNEERSOHN 181
Background 181
Jewish Unity 182
Body and Soul 183
The Holocaust 183
Israel 184
Education 184
Separation of Church and State 184
In Summation 185

JOSEPH B. SOLOVEITCHIK 187
Background 187
General Philosophy 188
Theology of Loneliness and the Split in Human Nature ... 189
Human Relationship to God 190
In Summation 190

HUMANISM AND ERIC FROMM   193
Background   193
Two Types of Religion   194
God: The Highest Value   195
Imitation of God   195
In Summation   196

RADICAL AMAZEMENT AND ABRAHAM
JOSHUA HESCHEL   197
Background   197
Philosophy of Religion   198
Heschel's Philosophy   199
The Meaning of Being Human   200
Ways to God   200
Heschel and Medieval Jewish Philosophy   202
In Summation   202

THEOLOGY AFTER THE HOLOCAUST   205
Moral Theories   205
Metaphysical Theories   206
Evil Is Temporary   206
Evil Is Inscrutable   206
Theodicy: Theologians' Responses to Evil in the World   207

RICHARD RUBENSTEIN   209
Background   209
"Death of God" Theology   209
Psychoanalytic Interpretation of Judaism   211
In Summation   212

ELIEZER BERKOVITS   213
Background   213
Responses to Suffering   214
Zionism   215
In Summation   216

IGNAZ MAYBAUM	217
Background	217
Response to Jewish Suffering	217
In Summation	219
EMIL FACKENHEIM	221
Background	221
Philosophy	221
Jewish History: "Root Experiences" and "Epoch-making Events"	222
In Summation	224
PHILOSOPHIES OF FOUR BRANCHES OF JUDAISM: ORTHODOX, REFORM, CONSERVATIVE, AND RECONSTRUCTIONIST	225
Orthodox Judaism	226
Background	226
Basic Jewish Philosophy and Beliefs	228
God	228
Torah and Revelation	228
The Jewish People and the Land of Israel	229
Reform Judaism	229
Background	229
Basic Jewish Philosophy and Beliefs	232
God	232
Torah	233
Mitzvot	233
The Jewish People	234
In Summation	235
Conservative Judaism	235
Background	235
Basic Jewish Philosophy and Beliefs	237
God	237
Revelation	237
Halachah—Jewish Law	238
The Jewish People and God's Election of Israel	239

The State of Israel and the Role of Religion   239
Social Justice   240
The Ideal Conservative Jew   240
Reconstructionist Judaism   241
Background   241
Basic Jewish Philosophy and Beliefs   242
God   242
Torah   242
The Jewish People   243
The Land of Israel   243
Social Action   244
In Summation   244

Glossary of Philosophic Terms   245

Further Reading   261

Index   263

PREFACE

While the foundational ideology of the Jew finds its roots in the Bible and its laws and customs, there are a variety of philosophic ideas and concepts that have developed throughout Jewish history that extend and transcend these basic ideas essential to Judaism. This book presents the reader with the philosophy and theology of great Jewish philosophers throughout the ages. Included are philosophers of the ancient, medieval, and modern periods, a brief biographical sketch of each of them, and their ideas and contribution to the world of Jewish philosophy. In addition, there is a chapter devoted to the philosophies of the four major branches of Judaism: Orthodox, Conservative, Reform, and Reconstructionist. A glossary of philosophic terms and philosophers and a list of books for further reading and research round out this volume.

I hope that the reader will be challenged by the panoply of ideas by these great thinkers who have contributed, each in his own way, to the rich philosophic culture of Judaism.

1

INTRODUCTION TO JEWISH PHILOSOPHY

Jewish philosophy is the interpretation of Jewish beliefs and practices using philosophic concepts and systems of understanding. Jewish philosophy arose and flourished as Jews began to participate in the philosophic speculations of the cultures in which they were immersed. The subject matter of Jewish philosophy includes the following: (1) philosophic study of unique aspects of Jewish tradition, including topics such as Jews as the chosen people, revelation, prophecy, the messiah, and the nature of afterlife; (2) issues common to Judaism, Christianity, and Islam, such as God's existence, God's divine attributes, the human soul, and principles of human conduct; and (3) topics of general philosophic interest, such as the structure of logical arguments and the nature of the universe.

Historically, Jewish philosophy is often divided into three periods: (1) its early development in the Diaspora community of the Hellenistic world, from the second century B.C.E. until the middle of the first century C.E.; (2) its thriving in Islamic and Christian countries during the Middle Ages (from the tenth to sixteenth centuries); and (3) the modern phase beginning in the eighteenth century and continuing to the present.

BIBLICAL AND RABBINIC ANTECEDENTS

Both the Bible and rabbinic literature contain explicit views about God, man, and the world. These views, however, are not presented in any formal systematic way, and thus it is more common to speak of biblical and rabbinic theology rather than philosophy. Nevertheless, Jewish philosophers throughout the ages often use and quote biblical and rabbinic sources in support of their various philosophic views.

Table 1–1 is a sampling of biblical verses concerning God and human nature that are often cited by Jewish philosophers in their works. Each verse is accompanied by its central message.

Table 1–1.

Biblical Verses Concerning God and Human Nature

Message	Verse
1. The One incomparable God	Hear O Israel, the Lord our God, the Lord is One. (Deuteronomy 6:4)
2. God creates and acts in the world	God said: Let there be light and there was light. (Genesis 1:3)
3. God is imageless	You saw no shape when the Lord your God spoke to you at Horeb out of the fire. (Deuteronomy 4:15)

4. Israel is God's chosen people	If you will listen to Me and keep My covenant, then you shall be My own treasure from among all peoples. (Exodus 19:4)
5. God has attributes	The Lord, the Lord God, merciful and gracious, long suffering and abundant in goodness and truth. . . . (Exodus 34:6)
6. Moses' prophecy was superior	Never again did there arise in Israel a prophet like Moses, whom God singled out, face to face. . . . (Deuteronomy 34:10)
7. God punishes wayward behavior	Be careful, lest your heart be deceived and you turn aside and worship other gods. And the anger of God be kindled against you, and He shut up the heaven. (Deuteronomy 11:16–17)
8. The heavens and the earth are finite	. . . from one end of the earth even unto the other end of the earth. (Deuteronomy 13:8)
9. God is omnipotent	I know that you canst do all things, and that no purpose of Yours can be thwarted. (Job 42:2)

10. Man possesses freedom of choice	I have set before you this day life and good, death and evil . . . therefore, choose life. . . . (Deuteronomy 30:15–19)
11. Man's essential nature is his reason	Let us make man in our image. (Genesis 1:26)
12. Man's final goal is love of God	Love the Lord with all your heart and all your soul. . . . (Deuteronomy 6:5)
13. Man should be modest in his conduct	Righteous eat to the satisfying of his desire. . . . (Proverbs 13:25)

RABBINIC LITERATURE

While the rabbis had some familiarity with Greek philosophic ideas because Greek philosophy had appeared by the time of the Talmud, research has shown that for the most part the rabbis were not familiar with formal philosophy. The names of the major philosophers are absent from the rabbinic writings, and the only philosophers mentioned by name are Epicurus and the obscure second-century Oenomaus of Gadara. In rabbinic literature the term epicurean (*apikoros*) is used, but it usually refers to a heretic rather than to someone who embraces Epicurus' doctrines. Jewish philosophers were prone to cite rabbinic sayings in their writings as they did biblical quotations, for support of their views. Table 1–2 is a brief listing of rabbinic quotations and the philosophic ideas that they represented.

Table 1–2.

Rabbinic Quotations and Philosophic Ideas

Rabbinic Quotation	Philosophic Idea
1. The Torah speaks in the language of the sons of man. (*Yevamot* 71a)	Attributes describing God in human terms must be understood as metaphor
2. All is in the hands of heaven except the fear of heaven. (Talmud *Berakhot* 33b)	Man has freedom of action
3. There is no death without sin, no sufferings without transgression. (*Shabbat* 55a)	Man's behavior affects his fate
4. In the World to come, there is no eating, no drinking, no washing, no anointing . . . but the righteous sit with crowns on their heads and enjoy the radiance of the Divine. (*Berakhot* 17a)	Spiritual nature of the afterlife
5. The world follows its customary order. (*Avodah Zarah* 54b)	A natural order exists in the world

2

SPIRITUAL MONOTHEISM AND PHILO JUDAEUS

THE BEGINNING OF JEWISH PHILOSOPHY

Jewish philosophy is said to have begun in the Diaspora community of the Hellenistic world during the second century B.C.E. and continued there until the first century C.E. It arose out of the confrontation between the Jewish religion and Greek philosophy and had as its aim the interpretation of Judaism in philosophic terms. It also had an apologetic purpose: to show that Judaism is a type of philosophy whose conception of God is a spiritual one and whose ethics are rational. Jewish philosophers polemicized against the polytheism of other religions and against pagan practices. In spite of their philosophic interests, they maintained that Judaism is superior to philosophy.

Philo of Alexandria is the only Jewish Hellenistic philosopher from whom a body of works has survived. All the other materials are either fragmentary or only allude to philosophic or theological topics. The language of Hellenistic Jewish philosophy was

Greek. Jewish Hellenistic culture may be said to have begun with the Septuagint, the Greek translation of the Bible.

The first Jewish philosopher appears to have been Aristobulus of Paneas (middle of the second century B.C.E.) who wrote a commentary on the *Five Books of Moses,* fragments of which have been preserved by Christian Church Fathers. He argued that Greek philosophers derived their teachings from the wisdom of Moses, and his interpretation of the Bible was an allegorical one. His essential premise in expounding the *Five Books of Moses* is that descriptions of God must be interpreted in a manner appropriate to God's nature. Thus, when the Bible applies to God expressions such as "hands," "arm," and "face," these are never to be understood literally. He cautioned against falling into the error of understanding divine matters anthropomorphically in the manner of mythology. He also maintained that wisdom (i.e., the Torah) existed prior to heaven and earth and that God's power extends through all things.

Of special interest is the interpretation given by Aristobulus to the expressions "standing" and "descending" as applied to God in the Bible. In his view, "standing" is a term connoting constancy and established order in natural phenomena, such as the regular succession of seasons. "Descending" signifies the revelation at Mount Sinai and the manifestation of God's glory to human beings on earth.

In Aristobulus' exposition of the creation story in the Bible, the number seven is very important. Not only did God rest on the seventh day, but God also instituted the seventh day as a day of rest for humans, in order that they would be free one day each week to contemplate the order and harmony of creation. This contemplation is accomplished by means of the intellect, man's seventh and most exalted faculty (the others being the five senses and the power of speech). Still further, the seven faculties of man correspond to the seven planets—evidence of the harmony between man and the universe as a whole.

PHILO JUDAEUS:
THE FATHER OF MEDIEVAL PHILOSOPHY

Philo Judaeus (c. 20 B.C.E. to c. 50 C.E.) of Alexandria is the most important figure in Jewish Hellenism and has been credited with being the true father of what was to become the medieval philosophic tradition. Although a devout Jew, he was well schooled in Greek philosophy and poetry.

Philo uses allegorical interpretation to a great extent in his explanation of the Bible. Indeed for him, the Bible has a plain meaning, and the events really did happen. But the Torah also has deeper meaning, telling us truths about human existence in every age. Thus, says Philo, when the Bible tells us that Abraham sent away his maidservant Hagar and remained with his wife Sarah (Genesis 21:8–14), it means that the good person, represented by Abraham, has to "send away," that is, to gain control over, physical desires, represented by Hagar, and heed the voice of reason and conscience, represented by Sarah.

The bulk of Philo's writings deal with the *Five Books of Moses*, which can be divided into three series of treatises. The first series consists of an exposition of the Five Books as a legal code. At the opening of the first book of the series, Philo explains that the *Five Books of Moses*, although a law code, opens with the story of creation rather than with legal material. For him this serves to demonstrate that the laws of the Bible are in harmony with the laws of nature. There follow biographies of the three Patriarchs (and Joseph), whom Philo interprets in accordance with Platonic theory as the living embodiments of the law or the archetypes on which the law was modeled by Moses.

The second is a philosophic interpretation of the *Five Books of Moses*. This series consists of eighteen exegetic treatises that parallel the first seventeen chapters of the Book of Genesis, completely disregarding their narrative content and transposing them by way of allegorization into a set of abstract philosophic-mystical concepts. The latter treatise draws its basic material from the various dream narratives of Genesis.

The third series, entitled Questions and Answers, consists of questions and answers on the Book of Exodus. It is in the form of a Hellenistic commentary, where each paragraph is headed by an exegetic question, answered by a short literal, and a lengthy allegorical, explanation.

GOD'S EXISTENCE

Philo was among the first of the Jewish thinkers to argue for the existence of God. In one of his well-known arguments, Philo asserts that just as a human being has a mind, so too does the universe have a Mind. And just as the human mind controls one's body, so must the universal Mind, namely God, control the universe.

In a second proof for God's existence (the so-called "teleological" argument based upon the design of the universe), Philo observes that there is an order and a design to the universe. Every design requires a designer. The organization and design of the universe, therefore, must have an organizing Mind behind it. The organizing Mind is none other than God.

GOD'S ESSENCE

In discussing God's essence, Philo maintains an extreme transcendentalism, describing God as a Unity that transcends virtue, knowledge, and even the good itself. Although God has no name and is unknowable, Philo maintains that one must strive to know God and that God is the only object worth knowing. According to Philo, God is the "soul" of the universe, the greatest cause of everything there is. Beyond all time and place, God fills the entire universe.

GOD'S NAME

Philo posited that unlike rabbinic and biblical literature, it was impossible, owing to the deficiency of language, to give God a precise name that would cover all aspects of God. Philo chose the word *Ontos* (Greek for "Being" or "that which exists") to refer to God.

Philo further posits that the only attributes one can apply to God are the negative ones. For example, to say that God is "holy" is simply not adequate, for this description would be limiting God to a person's idea of holiness. Thus for Philo, the most that one can say is that God in not unholy. The idea of Philo to use negative attributes in describing God is similar to that of Moses Maimonides, who will be described later in this volume.

GOD'S ONENESS

Greek philosophy played an important role in Philo's philosophic thinking. The Greeks held that human beings were composed of two major parts: body and soul. The body represents the material perishable aspect of life and that which is the foundation of evil. The soul, on the other hand, is representative of the rational mind that stands for eternal good.

A problem then arises, for the Book of Genesis (1:27) states that God created man in His own image. If man is composed of both a body and soul, it would then appear that God is also separated into these two distinct parts. Philo declared that the word "image" refers to the universal Mind after which peoples' minds are created. Thus, God remains a complete unity, indivisible and one.

GOD'S COMMUNICATION WITH PEOPLE

According to Philo, man is composed of body and soul, body connecting him with matter and soul with God. Thus, every person has to make a fundamental choice as to the direction of his life. In order to prepare himself for God, man has to strip himself of earthly bonds (i.e., his body and senses). Philo speaks of reaching God, using the three patriarchs (Abraham, Isaac, and Jacob) as the archetypes of the three main routes to uniting with God. The three routes are called learning, nature, and training. Abraham proceeds from learning (Hagar) to virtue (Sarah), whereas Isaac as the perfect nature reaches the mystical goal without interposing an intellectual endeavor, and Jacob is rewarded for his asceticism by the fact that the "Lord" (justice) becomes to him "God," meaning that God discloses to him His higher spheres.

There is an additional function of the doctrine of intermediaries. These intermediaries present themselves to the ascending soul as so many stages on its way to God. Although the soul is unable to advance to God Himself, it may be able to reach one of God's "powers," whose number is variously given. This is developed in an allegory of the six towns of refuge (Numbers 35), which are made to represent a sequel of stations on the way to God. The final goal is to reach the Divine Word.

In Jewish tradition, man is able to relate to God in two ways: in fear and in love. Philo, like the ancient rabbis, considers fear not only inferior to love, but sometimes as completely wrong, deriving from an inadequate idea of the Godhead. The proper attitude, he holds, is love to be directed to God.

GOD'S RELATION TO THE WORD—PHILO'S LOGOS

Although Philo asserted that God is incorporeal and beyond the limits of human understanding, he still maintained that God cared about the world and its people. He taught that God is able to operate in the world through the *logos* (Greek for "speech"), which at times he identified with the mind of God and at other times another name for God Himself. Although Philo taught that the world is created by God, God's direct contact with the defiling quality of matter is avoided by the interposition of the logos or world-creating power.

According to Plato, a prominent Greek philosopher of the fourth century B.C.E., everything in the world is a copy of the perfect essence of that particular object or thing. Objects themselves will eventually perish, but the essence or form is eternal. Thus, for example, all the tables in the world have an eternal form that is independent even of God. God contemplates the essence and creates the object.

Philo was influenced by Plato's theory of forms but did not accept these forms as eternal patterns existing outside of God. He did hold that these forms were not eternal but were created by God.

With regard to creation, Philo maintained that it was carried out in two successive stages, as illustrated in the biblical narrative. The first day of creation represents God's conceiving in His logos the world of ideas that served as a model for the creation of the material world, represented by the other five days. In the creation of man, the only creature capable of doing evil, God needs the cooperation of subservient powers.

THE PROBLEM OF EVIL

Philo asserted that the world's evils emerge from the world of matter, a consequence of the imperfection of the world. In certain instances, though, God is the cause of evil. Such is the case when God inflicted punishment upon the Egyptians in the time of Moses and the exodus from Egypt.

Regarding the suffering of righteous people, Philo closely

followed the rabbinic thinkers of his time, who argued that the righteous sometimes suffer because their righteousness is not perfect. In addition, evil may be seen as a test of lack of faith. And finally, people sometimes suffer because of the transgressions of their ancestors rather than as a consequence of their own sins.

MAN AS A MORAL BEING

Most important in Philo's system is the doctrine of the moral development of man. Of this he distinguishes two conditions: that before time was, and that since the beginning of time. In the pretemporal condition, the soul is without body, free from earthly matter, without sex, in the condition of the generic man, morally perfect and without flaws, but still striving after a higher purity. On entering upon time the soul loses its purity as it is confined to the body. The *nous* (mind), as Philo refers to it, becomes earthly, but it retains a tendency toward something higher. Philo is not entirely certain whether the body in itself is evil. It clearly is a source of danger as it is able to drag the spirit into the bonds of sensibility. For Philo, sensibility is the source of man's passion and desires.

According to Philo, man passes through several steps in his ethical development. At first the several elements of the human being are in a state of latency, presenting a kind of moral neutrality that Philo designates by the terms "naked" or "medial." In this period of moral indecision God endeavors to prepare the earthly nous for virtue, presenting to him an image of earthly wisdom and virtue. Man quickly leaves this state of neutrality, for as soon as he meets the woman (sensibility), he is filled with desire, and passion ensnares his entire being.

According to Philo there are three methods whereby one can rise toward the divine: through teaching, through practice, and through natural goodness. Teaching includes a student studying grammar, geometry, astronomy, and logic. The highest stage of teaching is philosophy, which begins to divide finite knowledge from infinite knowledge. Here a person begins to understand that the only subject of contemplation for the wise is ethics. By the method of practice man strives to attain the highest good by means of moral action.

The final method with which a person can rise toward the divine is through natural goodness. Philo cites the biblical Isaac as an example of good disposition.

IN SUMMATION

Philo, borrowing from Plato's theory of forms, was able to balance a transcendentalist view of God with a strong immanentistic trend based on the logos, allowing the spiritual God to operate in the material world. For Philo, God exists and is unknowable. It is the challenge of human beings to develop their powers of reason in order to "reach" God.

Philo emphasized God's special relation with the Israelite nation, stating that the gift of having a vision of God was given to the entire people of Israel. Furthermore, the revelation of the Torah was God's special gift to Israel, for Israel has been favored by God with the highest level of prophecy.

Few ancient Jewish sources mention Philo in their writings, although there are traces of his influence in the *Midrash*. The first medieval Jewish writer to mention him is Azariah dei Ross (Me'or Einayim [1886], pp. 90–129) who Hebraicizes his name into Yedidya. Philo had a much greater influence on Christianity, specifically for the Church Fathers. They drew on his allegorical interpretations and adopted many of his concepts, including that of the logos.

3

MEDIEVAL JEWISH PHILOSOPHY

Medieval Jewish philosophy began in the early tenth century as part of a general cultural revival in the Islamic East and continued in Muslim countries—North Africa, Spain, and Egypt—for some 300 years. The Jews of this period spoke, read, and wrote Arabic and were able to participate in the general culture of their day. The major speculative efforts of the Jewish philosophy of this period were devoted to investigating how Judaism and philosophy were related.

At the end of the twelfth century the Jewish communities in the Islamic world declined. Hebrew now became the language of Jewish works, and Jews began to produce an extensive literature devoted to purely philosophic topics. The second period in medieval Jewish philosophy lasted until the early sixteenth century.

Jewish philosophers of the Islamic period may be divided into four groups: followers of the Mutazilite branch of the Kalam, Neoplatonists, Aristotelians, and philosophic critics of Aristotelian rationalism. Following is a brief summary of each of these groups.

MUTAZILITE KALAM

Mutazilite Kalam arose toward the end of the eighth century. Its views developed out of reflections on problems posed by the Bible. The two major problems were the unity of God and God's justice. The first problem arose because the Koran observed that God is one yet described God by many attributes. The second problem resulted from the observation that God is omnipotent and omniscient (which seems to imply that God causes human actions), and yet God punishes man for his wrongdoing. To solve the first problem the Mutazilites set out to show that God can be described by many attributes without violating His unity. To solve the second problem, although God is all-knowing and all-powerful, man's freedom and hence responsibility for his actions are not precluded. Mutazilites also dealt with the nature of different kinds of transgressors and the afterlife. Unlike the Neoplatonists and Aristotelians, since the Mutazilites used philosophy to solve biblical difficulties, they did not have a need to formulate a systematic philosophy.

NEOPLATONISM

Neoplatonism was characterized by the doctrine of emanation, which posits that the world and its parts emanated from a first principle, God, in a manner analogous to the emanation of rays from the sun. To safeguard the unity of God, Neoplatonists posited a first emanation identified by some with wisdom (logos) and by others with will, which was between God and the world. They also posited a number of spiritual substances— intellect, soul, and nature—between the first emanation and the world.

Neoplatonists also maintained that God is completely above the created order and can be described only by negative attributes. They generally subscribed to the duality of body and soul, and to man's purpose in life to free the soul from the body, thus making it possible for it to rejoin the upper region from whence it came. This was to be accomplished through practice of moral virtues and through philosophic speculation.

ARISTOTELIANISM

Aristotelianism was based on the premises that the world must be known through observation and that this knowledge is gained through study of the various speculative and practical sciences. Logic is the prerequisite instrument of all of the sciences. Aristotelian physics is based on an analysis of changes in the world, which are explained through the four causes: the material, the efficient, the formal, and the final causes. The world is divided into the celestial and the sublunar regions. In the sublunar world there is corruption, whereas the celestial region is not subject to corruption.

For Aristotelians, all organic beings—plants, animals, and human—are governed by an internal principle of motion called a soul. In a human being, the soul possesses nutritive, sensory, appetitive, imaginative, and rational powers. The highest faculty is the rational, and to develop it is the ultimate purpose of life itself. The agent in the production of human knowledge is called the active intellect, which also produces prophecy in men who have the required preparation. Morality for Aristotelians is the acquisition of the moral and intellectual virtues.

CRITICS OF ARISTOTELIANISM

The critical reaction to philosophy was marked by an attempt to show, on philosophic grounds, that philosophers had not made good their claim to have discovered physical and metaphysical truths. The fact that philosophers could not agree on these truths was taken as evidence that they had failed. However, while the critics rejected physics and metaphysics, they accepted the principles of Aristotelian logic.

4

SAADIA GAON: THE FIRST PHILOSOPHER OF THE MIDDLE AGES

BACKGROUND

Born in 882 in Pithom, Egypt, Saadia Gaon is considered one of the greatest authors and scholars of the Geonic period and an important leader of Babylonian Jewry. *Geonim* (singular *gaon,* meaning genius in modern Hebrew) were the heads of the Babylonian *yeshivot* from the eighth century, serving as spiritual leaders for all Babylonian Jewry. Saadia was a *gaon* and the first medieval Jewish philosopher. From 921 Saadia appears as the leading protagonist in an ongoing struggle between Aaron ben Meir, head of the Jerusalem academy, and the leaders of the Babylonian Jewish communities. The cause of the struggle was a technicality over the fixing of the calendar, although the large issue at stake was whether the sages of Palestine or Babylonia were to be the chief leaders of world Jewry.

In 922, after arriving in Babylonia, Saadia was appointed head of the yeshivah of Pumbedita. In 928 he was appointed head of the Sura academy.

Saadia was a pioneer of rabbinic literature. He was also the first to give his halakhic works the form of monographs, assigning a separate one to each topic of Jewish law. He was likewise also the first to set a standard pattern for his books of legal decisions by dividing each one into sections and subsections. Every subject begins with a brief definition of the topic under discussion, followed by various details and Talmudic proofs of them. Saadia was also the first to write halakhic works in Arabic, which had in his day replaced Aramaic as the language spoken by the Babylonian Jews.

Saadia is most renowned for his *Book of Beliefs and Opinions (Sefer Emunot ve-Deiot)*, the first systematic philosophical explanation of Judaism. He also translated the Bible into Arabic and prepared a uniform prayer book for the Jews living in the Arab world.

Saadia's last years were peaceful, and he died in 942.

SAADIA THE HALAKHIST

The largest and most important part of Saadia's Jewish legal work consists of monographs on halakhic decisions, which covered most of what is at present included in the Choshen Mishpat of the Code of Jewish Law, as well as books on ritual purity and impurity, incest, festivals, and the proclamation of the new month.

Saadia goes into the fullest details of every halakhic topic he touches on, but he frequently omits entire "Halachot," which have a direct bearing on the subject at issue, either because he thought of dealing with them within the context of some other halakhic monograph, or because he regarded them as too unimportant to be included in the discussion. Saadia's halakhic books are distinguished by their systematic structure and logical order and by a detailed introduction that he prefaced to each book.

PHILOSOPHY

Saadia's major philosophic work, written in Arabic, is the earliest Jewish philosophic work from medieval times to have survived intact. In 1186 it was translated into Hebrew by Judah ibn Tibbon under the title *Sefer ha-Emunot VehaDe'ot (Book of Beliefs and Opinions)*. In this volume Saadia set out to find rational proof for the dogmas of the Oral and Written Law. Saadia's importance lies in his being the first medieval Jewish philosopher to reconcile the Bible and philosophy, reason and revelation.

Saadia identifies three sources of knowledge: sense perception, self-evident principles (such as the approval of telling the truth and the disapproval of lying), and inferential knowledge gained by syllogistic reasoning. Saadia goes on to identify a fourth source of knowledge: reliable tradition (i.e., confidence in the truth of the reports of others). In Judaism, reliable tradition has special significance in that it refers to the transmission, through the Bible and the oral tradition, of God's revelation to the prophets. Saadia maintains that revelation is crucial in order to impart the truth to those who are incapable of rational investigation.

Saadia also sees a correspondence between reason and revelation and states that one cannot refute the other. Thus Saadia maintains that one must reject the validity of any prophet whose teachings contradict reason.

THEORY OF THE WORLD

Saadia maintains that the world was created in time, *ex nihilo*, and that its creator was other than itself. He presents the four proofs for creation. In the first, he concludes that the force preserving the world is finite and, consequently, that the world itself must be finite (i.e., must have a beginning and an end). In the second proof, on the basis of the fact that what is composed of two or more elements must have been put together at some point in time, Saadia argues that the world, which is composed of various elements, must have been created at some point in time. In the third proof, Saadia argues that the world is composed of various substances, all of which are the bearers of accidents. Since accidents originate in time, the world itself must have originated in time. The fourth argument is taken for the nature of time. Were the world uncreated, time would be infinite. But infinite time cannot be traversed, and hence the present moment could never have come to be. But the present clearly exists, and thus time cannot be infinite. Therefore it follows that the world must have a beginning.

Having advanced these four proofs of creation, Saadia then proceeds to refute all other cosmogonic theories that differ from his own.

NATURE OF GOD

Saadia's concept of God's nature is based on his view of God as creator. God, he maintains, is the cause of all corporeal existence. God cannot be corporeal, for if He were, there would have to be something beyond Him which was the cause of His existence. Since God is incorporeal, God cannot be subject of the corporeal attributes of quantity and number and hence cannot be more than one.

Regarding divine attributes, Saadia emphasizes three essential qualities of God: life, power, and wisdom. For Saadia, the creation of the world itself by God was an act of free will. In creating the world, God wanted to benefit His creatures by giving them the opportunity of serving Him through the observances of His commandments, by means of which they could attain true happiness.

MITZVOT

Saadia categorizes God's laws into rational laws (*mitzvot sichliyot*),which have their basis in reason, and the traditional ritual and ceremonial laws (*mitzvot shimiyot*), such as the dietary laws (i.e., kashrut), which do not have their basis in reason. The acts to which the traditional laws refer are neither good nor evil from the point of view of reason, but are made so by the fact that they are commanded or prohibited by God. All rational laws are subsumed under three rational principles: first, reason demands that one thank one's benefactor. Hence, it is reasonable that God should demand that a person thank Him through worship. Second, reason demands that a wise person not permit himself to be insulted. Hence, it is reasonable that God should prohibit man from insulting Him. Third, reason demands that creatures should not harm each other. Hence it is reasonable that God prohibit people from stealing and murdering.

In order for man to arrive at knowledge of both the traditional and rational laws, revelation is necessary.

THE NATURE OF MAN

Saadia maintains that man is composed of body and soul. The soul, composed of very fine material, has three essential faculties: appetite, which controls growth and reproduction; spirit, which controls the emotions; and reason, which controls knowledge. A soul cannot act on its own; therefore, it is placed in the body which serves as its instrument. By means of the performance of the *mitzvot* (divine commandments), man can attain true happiness.

Man also has freedom of choice, for if he did not, he would not be responsible for his actions. Saadia further maintains that although God knows what the outcome of a person's deliberations will be, God does not cause a person to act in a specific way.

Regarding the question of theodicy (i.e., why the evil prosper and righteous suffer), Saadia maintains a traditional rabbinic view that states that the righteous who suffer in this world will be rewarded in a world to come. Regarding the soul, Saadia argues that it remains in a sort of limbo-like state until it will be reunited with the body at the time of the messiah.

SAADIA AS LITURGIST

Since in his time there was no methodically arranged prayer book, Saadia took it upon himself to compile the prayers for the whole year. Entitled *Collection of All Prayers and Praises*, it was well known in Egypt and in other Arab-speaking countries. Saadia also composed numerous Piyyutim (liturgical poems) as well as penitential prayers. He was among the first to write philosophic liturgical poems that were to serve as a model for such Spanish poets as Solomon ibn Gabirol and Judah Halevi.

IN SUMMATION

Saadia is clearly one of the dominant figures in the development of Judaism and its literature. He is the most authoritative Geonic source. He influenced numerous Jewish Neoplatonists, such as Bachya ibn Pakuda and Moses ibn Ezra. He was also a pioneer of rabbinic literature, one of the first to write "books" in the modern sense of the word. His halakhic monographs continue to be studied by Talmud students throughout the world.

5

NEOPLATONISM: SOLOMON IBN GABIROL

BACKGROUND

The main source of information on Gabirol's life is his poems. He was said to have been born in Málaga (c.1020) but as a child was taken to Saragossa, where he acquired an extensive education. He began writing poetry at a young age. One of his important supporters was Yekutiel ben Isaac ibn Chasan, whom he praised in a number of poems for his knowledge of the Talmud and the sciences.

It is thought that Gabirol wrote "Tikkun Middot HaNefesh" ("Improvement of the Moral Qualities") in 1045, and soon afterward he seems to have left Saragossa. From then on few details are available on his life and work. According to ibn Ezra, Gabirol died in Valencia at the age of 30,but Abraham ben David states that he died in 1070, when he was approximately 50 years old.

PHILOSOPHY

Gabirol presents his philosophy in his major work *Mekor Chayim* (*The Source of Life*). This work is composed in the form of a dialogue between master and student. The student's questions serve to enable the master to expound his views.

Mekor Chayim is divided into five treatises. The first treatise is devoted primarily to a discussion of the principles of matter and form as they exist in the objects of sense perception.

The second treatise contains a description of the spiritual matter that underlies corporeal form. The third is devoted to demonstrating the existence of simple substances. The fourth deals with the form and matter of simple substances, and the fifth, with universal form and matter as they exist in themselves.

Gabirol's cosmological system has a Neoplatonic structure with some modifications. The first principle is the First Essence, which can be identified with God. Next in order of being are the divine will, universal matter and form, then the simple substances—intellect, soul, and nature—and finally the corporeal world and its parts.

Gabirol maintains that all substances in the world, both spiritual and corporeal, are composed of two elements: form and matter. This duality produces the differences between the various substances. All distinctions between matter and form in the various substances stem from the distinction between universal matter and universal form, the most general kinds of matter and form which, according to Gabirol's account of being, are the first created things. However, Gabirol presents divergent accounts of their creation.

According to one account, universal matter comes from the essence of God, and form comes from the divine will. According to another account, both of these principles were created by the divine will.

All forms, according to Gabirol, in addition to appearing in various levels of being, are also contained in universal form. Matter and form do not exist by themselves. Their first compound is intellect, the first of the spiritual substances, from which the soul emanates. The soul is emanated from intellect, and there are three kinds of them: rational, animate, and vegetative. Nature, as a cosmic principle, emanates from the vegetative soul. It is, according to Gabirol, the last of the simple substances, and from it emanates corporeal substance, which is below nature in the order of being.

For the soul to be joined to a body, a mediating principle is required. The mediating principle is the heavens: the mediating principle joining the rational soul of man to the body is the animal spirit.

Above the knowledge of form and matter there is a far more sublime knowledge, namely that of the divine will, which is identical with divine wisdom. In its function as the efficient cause of everything, it unites form with matter.

Gabirol maintains that the goal to which all people should aspire is knowledge of the purpose for which they were created.

ETHICS

Gabirol's work in the area of ethics was entitled *Tikkun Middot HaNefesh*, written about 1045. In this volume, Gabirol discusses the parallel between the universe, the macrocosmos, and man, the microcosmos. Gabirol developed an original theory in which each of twenty personal traits is assigned to one of the five senses: pride, meekness, modesty, and impudence are related to the sense of sight; love, mercy, hate, and cruelty, to the sense of hearing; anger, goodwill, envy, and diligence, to the sense of smell; joy, anxiety, contentedness, and regret, to the sense of taste; and generosity, stinginess, courage, and cowardice, to the sense of touch. Gabirol also describes the relation between the virtues and the four qualities (heat, cold, moistness, and dryness), which are incorporated in pairs in each of the four elements of which the earth is composed: earth, air, water, and fire.

POETRY

In his poetic works, Gabirol displays his extensive knowledge of biblical Hebrew, Talmud, and Midrash and Arab poetry. His scientific knowledge, especially his mastery of astronomy, is evident in his writings as well.

Most of Gabirol's secular poetry was composed in honor of patrons. In his specifically ethical poems, Gabirol addresses the reader directly, propounding an ethic based upon individual introspection. These poems deal with the transience of life and the worthlessness of bodily existence as compared to the eternal values of spiritual life and the immortality of the soul.

Gabirol composed many liturgical poems as well, many of which have been preserved in both Sephardic and Ashkenazic prayer books. The famous prayer *Adon Olam* (Eternal God) has often been attributed to Gabirol. It is on the basis of these poems that Gabirol is regarded as the major religious poet of Spanish Jewry.

Although Gabirol's God is a personal one, to whom he may turn in supplication, he does not (as did Judah Halevi) describe his great love for God as the relationship between the lover and the beloved.

The concepts in Gabirol's mystical poems are very difficult to reconcile with the philosophic concepts expressed in his other works. In these poems, knowledge of the Divinity can be understood only by the elect who have plumbed the mysteries of creation. Some have said that Gabirol may have written many of these poems when in a state of ecstasy.

IN SUMMATION

As one of Spain's major religious poets, Gabirol's liturgical poems have left a lasting mark on Jewish liturgy. Many of them continue to appear in modern Ashkenazic and Sephardic prayer books. His philosophic work *Mekor Chayim* is unique in the body of Jewish philosophic-religious literature of the Middle Ages, because it expounds a complete philosophic-religious system wholly lacking in specifically Jewish content and terminology. The work is often quoted by Jewish philosophers, including the likes of Moses ibn Ezra and Abraham ibn Ezra. Gabirol also influenced Christian thought extensively, primarily through Latin translations of his major works.

6

BACHYA IBN PAKUDA

BACKGROUND

Bachya ibn Pakuda is the best known of all Jewish moral philosophers. There is relatively little known about the details of his life beyond the fact that he lived in Muslim Spain, probably at Saragossa. Bachya was also known as a *paytan* and wrote a variety of liturgical poems. His major work, *Kitab al-Hidaya ila Faraid al-Qulub*, was written around 1080. It was later translated into Hebrew by Judah ibn Tibbon in 1161 under the title *Hovot ha-Levavot (Duties of the Heart)*. In this work Bachya drew a great deal upon non-Jewish sources, even borrowing from Muslim mysticism and Arab Neoplatonism. This work established itself as the single most important Jewish ethical treatise of the whole medieval and early modern period.

DUTIES OF THE HEART

Bachya's *Duties of the Heart* is often considered the first systematic presentation of the ethics of Judaism. In it, Bachya describes the Jewish faith as a great spiritual truth founded on reason, revelation, and tradition. The book is modeled after the works of Muslim mysticism, which attempts to lead the reader through the various ascending stages of man's inner life toward spiritual perfection and finally communion with God. *Duties of the Heart* is divided into 10 "gates" (chapters), each of which is devoted to a particular duty of the heart, which the Jew must observe if he is to attain spiritual perfection. The 10 chapters deal with the affirmation of the unity of God, the nature of the world disclosing the workings of God, divine worship, trust in God, sincerity of purpose, humility, repentance, self-examination, asceticism, and the love of God.

Combining depth of emotion, poetic imagination, eloquence, and exquisite diction with a keen intellect, Bachya appeals to the sentiments and stirs the hearts of his readers. He declares that a person may be as holy as an angel and yet will not equal the one who leads a fellow person to righteousness.

Bachya's great personality, rich in piety and touching humility, shines through every line of his *Duties of the Heart*. In his chapter on humility, he declares that humility is expressed in gentle conduct toward fellow men, whether or not they are of equal standing. It springs from a consideration of one's own failings and shortcomings. Humility is shown especially of one's own failings and shortcomings.

Faith, Bachya maintains, must be intellectual, not blind and unreasoning. God's existence is knowable from the fact that nonexistent beings cannot create existent beings. Tradition alone, without the support of scientific proof, is sufficient for those who are not able to study. But, Bachya maintains, if one is a person of intellect, that person is obligated to use his faculties to gain a definitive knowledge of the truth.

The first division of *Duties of the Heart* includes the various ritual and ethical observances commanded by the Torah. These include the observance of the Sabbath, prayer, and the giving of charity. The second division of the book consists of beliefs, including belief in the existence of God, God's unity and spiritual traits (e.g., trust in God, love and fear of God, and repentance). The prohibitions against bearing a grudge and taking revenge are also examples of duties of the heart.

Bachya explained that he wrote this book because the duties of man's inner life had been neglected by his predecessors and contemporaries whose writings had concentrated on religious observances. To remedy this deficiency, Bachya wrote *Duties of the Heart*, which may be considered a kind of counterpart to the legal compendia of his predecessors and contemporaries.

MAN'S SOUL AND THE COMMANDMENTS

In accordance with Platonic teachings, Bachya maintains that man's soul, which is celestial in origin, is placed by divine decree within the body, where it runs the risk of forgetting its mission. The human soul is assisted by the intellect and revealed Law in order to achieve its goal. To elucidate this point, Bachya distinguishes between rational and traditional commandments. He asserts that the duties of the members of the body may be divided into rational commandments and traditional religious commandments, while the duties of the heart are all rooted in the intellect. With the assistance of reason and the revealed Law, the soul can triumph over its enemy.

WORSHIP OF THE DIVINE

In the third chapter of *Duties of the Heart*, Bachya discusses divine worship, which he defines as the expression of man's gratitude to God. To fulfill his duties to God without faltering, man must diligently practice a number of virtues. One of these is trust in God, which is based on the belief that God is good and has the power to protect man. To trust in God does not mean that one should neglect one's work, but rather that one should attempt to diligently carry out one's duties, trusting that God will remove obstacles along the way. While man has the freedom to will and choose, the realization of his actions is dependent on God's will. Further, a sound spiritual life requires a true correspondence between man's conscience and his behavior. Virtuous behavior includes humility, repentance, and temperance. For Bachya, the highest stage of the spiritual life is the love of God.

IN SUMMATION

Bachya's *Duties of the Heart* established itself as the single most important Jewish ethical treatise of the whole medieval and modern period. His philosophy was largely Neoplatonic, and his asceticism has strong spiritual affinities with the Arab mystics. Bachya profoundly influenced subsequent Jewish moralists, mystics, and ethicists.

7

JUDAH HALEVI: POET-PHILOSOPHER EXTRAORDINAIRE

BACKGROUND

It is believed that Judah Halevi was born in Tudela to a wealthy and learned family. At an early age he participated in poetry contests and won a competition of imitating a complicated poem by Moses ibn Ezra. Ibn Ezra developed a close relationship with him. In Granada, Halevi wrote his first important poems—eulogies and poetic letters—as well as wine and love poems.

With the coming of the Almoravides from Africa and their conquest of Muslim Spain, the position of the Jews in Andalusia deteriorated, and Judah Halevi left Granada. For the following twenty years he traveled through numerous Jewish communities. In Toledo, he practiced medicine in the service of the king and his nobles. Aside from his profession as a physician, he also engaged in trade with Jewish merchants in Egypt.

Of all his ties with various people, Judah Halevi's friendship with Abraham ibn Ezra was especially long-lasting. In his biblical commentaries, ibn Ezra quotes Halevi numerous times in matters of grammar and philosophy.

Halevi's greatest philosophic volume was entitled *The Kuzari: A Book of Argument in Defense of a Despised Religion.* It is named after the king of the Khazars in the country of Khazaria (located between Russia and Turkey). The king's conversion to Judaism provides the literary framework of the work. The book is passionate about the Jews' need to return to their spiritual homeland of Israel. At the book's conclusion, the Jewish spokesman informs the king that he is planning to emigrate to Israel. Likewise, late in his own life, Halevi left Spain and moved to Israel. In many ways, he had been prepared to go there for much of his life. "My heart is in the East," he had written in his famous poem, "but I am in the ends of the West." It is said that Halevi was killed by an Arab horseman soon after he arrived in Jerusalem.

THE KUZARI

The Kuzari, the great philosophic work of Judah Halevi, is regarded as one of the classics of Judaism. Its chief purpose is to show that the continuity of Jewish tradition is the best proof of the validity of the Jewish faith. Written in the form of a discussion at the court of the king of the Khazars, who embraced the Jewish religion in the seventh century, the Kuzari vindicates Judaism against the assaults of its various detractors.

The salient teachings of the book are: the good life is the aim of religion; Judaism, the religion of joy, imposes limits on asceticism; the good person will not shun the world and its activities; Israel is the heart of humanity, filling the same function in the world at large as does the heart in the body of man; Israel, the martyr-people, feels every pain and disorder of the great body of humanity; the Jewish people have been dispersed throughout the world in order to disseminate the divine truth; Israel has a special aptitude for prophecy by virtue of its Torah and ancestry; man possesses free will and is master of his choice;

and God knows the consequences of human actions, but this is not equivalent to foreordaining them.

The Kuzari is divided into five parts. In the first part, the philosopher, the Christian, and the Muslim expound their views. The king is with the philosopher, and when he realizes that Christianity and Islam are both based on Judaism, he calls in a Jewish scholar. The following four parts of the book are devoted to a dialogue between the king and the Jew.

In the second part, the king questions the Jewish scholar concerning the attributes of God. The scholar, however, is more concerned with the experience of God gained through prophecy than with the theoretical knowledge of God. He directs the discussion to the circumstances in which prophecy arose, and to the particular qualities of the land of Israel, its people, and language.

The third part deals with the details of the worship of God in Judaism. The scholar explains that Jewish worship consists of the fulfillment of the biblical commandments, which originated in divine revelation. The only way in which they can be interpreted is by means of the authoritative tradition. The last point leads to a detailed argument against Karaism (i.e., a Jewish doctrine that rejects rabbinic interpretation and bases its tenets on the literal interpretation of the Bible).

In the fourth part, the scholar discusses the names of God, distinguishing between the terms *Elohim* and *Adonai*. *Elohim* is understood as a general term denoting the God who is known through philosophic reasoning, whereas *Adonai* is a proper name, denoting the God of Israel who is known only through revelation and prophecy. Prophecy is explained as the experience of being in God's presence. The scholar goes on to say that only the people of Israel possess the faculty of prophecy.

The fifth and last part of the book is a polemic with the philosopher whom he did not properly challenge in the first part. The Jewish scholar presents his student with a sketch of the

Aristotelian philosophy of his day, at the same time exposing its weakness.

PROPHECY

Halevi's teachings are based on the concept of immediate religious experience and its superiority over deductive reasoning. However, he does not negate the value of metaphysical speculation, recognizing that in the absence of direct experience it is the only way of learning the truth.

Regarding prophecy, Halevi defines the prophet as one who, by means of a special "inner sense," is able to comprehend spiritual reality in the same way that the ordinary man, by means of the external senses, apprehends physical reality. Because the prophet can directly experience the presence of God, he can become much closer to God than the philosopher who only has an indirect theoretical knowledge of God. According to Halevi, the mission of the prophet is not to instruct people in eternal truths, but to teach them the deeds whose performance leads to the experience of God's presence. This is also the purpose of the Torah.

For Halevi, the prophetic faculty is hereditary and unique to the Jewish people. The prophets are able to bring God's presence closer to the people.

CRITICISM OF CHRISTIANITY AND ISLAM

Halevi asserts that Judaism, a prophetic religion, has no need to verify itself by means of rational proof. When Halevi objects to Christianity and Islam, he is in fact objecting to the fact that these religions cannot base their doctrines on an unambiguous historical revelation that allowed 600 Israelites at Mount Sinai to be granted the experience of prophecy. Thus, Halevi posits, Christianity and Islam must resort to the historical tradition of

Judaism. Halevi recognizes the presence of authentic Jewish elements in both Christianity and Islam and the important role that they have played in history. However, since they have diverged from the Torah and sought to displace it, they are falsehoods that cannot claim authentic historical validity.

HALEVI'S CONCEPT OF "DIVINE INFLUENCE"

Halevi uses the technical term *Ha-Inyan ha-Elohi* ("divine influence") in his writings. Divine influence refers to an intermediary between man and God. It was initially known to the patriarchs Abraham, Isaac, and Jacob and then to the entire people of Israel. For Halevi, Israel's history is the only true history of humankind as demonstrated by the fact that only in the history of the people of Israel is divine providence directly manifest. When the other nations of the world recognize the divine influence, they too, says Halevi, will become a part of the true history.

For Halevi, the suffering of the people of Israel is not evidence of the inferiority of Jewish faith, but rather of its superiority. Halevi asserts that such suffering is tantamount to the public sanctification of God's name, and its true purpose will be understood at the time of deliverance and redemption.

HALEVI'S POEMS

Halevi wrote hundreds of poems covering a range of subjects. His love poems, which number about 80, are addressed to a deer or to a gazelle or—as marriage poems—to the two together.

The largest number of Judah Halevi's secular poems deal with eulogy and friendship. The majority of these poems were written for his famous contemporaries: poets, philosophers, and religious scholars (e.g., Moses ibn Ezra).

Halevi also composed many Piyyutim: liturgical poems for

Jewish festivals. Job's lament, the cries of Lamentations, and the bitter complaints of the Prophet Jeremiah are resounding themes in his Piyyutim. Depression resulting from the delay of redemption is expressed in several of his liturgical poems.

Along with Piyyutim of a national nature on such biblical and historic themes as the description of the miracles in Egypt in the poems of Passover and the miracle of Purim are found lyric poems expressing personal religious experiences. In these poems Halevi expresses man's reverence for God and his dread of transgression. He also writes of his happiness with God and his devotion to Him.

Perhaps the most famous of the poetic works of Judah Halevi are the "Shirei Tziyon" ("Poems of Zion"). Some of these poems express the theme of longing for the Land of Israel. Others were written on his voyage to the Land of Israel in which the story of the Mediterranean Sea and the final calm is described in graphic detail.

Halevi's poems were widespread in manuscript from an early period. During his lifetime they were already known outside of Spain. From the beginning of printing, many were included in various festival prayer books and liturgical books of penitential prayer.

IN SUMMATION

Halevi's book *The Kuzari*, in the Hebrew translation of Judah ibn Tibbon, was of great influence among Jewish readers and is regarded as one of the classics of Judaism. It was particularly influential in kabbalistic circles in the thirteenth century and among the anti-Aristotelians in the fourteenth and fifteenth centuries. In more recent times it had a marked influence on Hasidism. Halevi's many poems continue to be read and studied throughout the world.

8

ARISTOTELIANISM: ABRAHAM BEN DAVID HALEVI IBN DAUD

BACKGROUND

Ibn Daud was a Spanish historian and philosopher born toward the beginning of the twelfth century. Though little is known of his early life, it is clear that he received a well-rounded education that included rabbinics, Bible, Hebrew poetry, and Greek and Jewish philosophy. In the wake of the Almohad conquest of Spain, ibn Daud fled to Castile where he settled in Toledo, the city with which he was most deeply associated, until his death in 1180.

Ibn Daud's major historical work, *Sefer HaKabbalah* (*Book of Tradition*), was written from 1160 to 1161, the very same year in which his philosophic treatise *Al 'Aqida al-Rafia* was written. Both were polemical works, the one defending Judaism through history and the other through philosophy.

PHILOSOPHY

Ibn Daud was the first Jewish philosopher to introduce a strict form of Aristotelianism. This type of philosophy had already become dominant among Muslims, but Jewish thinkers still followed Neoplatonism. In taking this step toward Aristotelianism, ibn Daud was the precursor of Moses Maimonides.

Ibn Daud was one of the most rationalistic of Jewish philosophers. In his view, true philosophy is in complete harmony with the Torah, because the Torah contains everything brought to light by human reason subsequent to revelation. He maintains that the acquisition of metaphysical knowledge is the real purpose of man. He therefore focuses on the philosophic interpretation of religious concepts.

GOD

Ibn Daud subscribed to the Aristotelian proof of God known as the proof of the Prime Mover. This proof holds that all motion requires a moving cause, and since the sequence of causes cannot regress infinitely, it must have its origin in a first unmoved mover (i.e., God). To this proof, ibn Daud adds one formulated by Avicenna known as the proof from necessity and contingency. According to this proof, the existence of all beings other than God is contingent, not necessary, and contingent beings must have their origin in a being necessary through itself, who is God.

Following Islamic Aristotelians, he deduces from the necessary existence of God His absolute unity and uniqueness, because any plurality in God would require the existence beyond Him of a unifying principle, which would contradict God's necessary existence. Ibn Daud deduces God's uniqueness, because the absolute unity of God precludes the existence of two different necessary beings, and two completely like beings would necessarily have to be identical. Thus he reaches the Neoplatonic concept of God as the absolute One. With this concept of God's unity in the sense of simplicity, ibn Daud had to reject the possibility of any positive attributes of God and maintain that God is unknowable in any positive fashion.

THE SOUL, PROPHECY, AND FREE WILL

Like Avicenna, ibn Daud maintained that the Aristotelian definition of the soul as the form of an organic body does not necessarily imply that the existence of the human soul is dependent upon the existence of body, as are all other forms. The human soul is capable of continuing after death without the body because the activities of the intellect are independent of the body altogether.

Regarding prophecy, ibn Daud adopted a naturalistic interpretation. He regards prophecy as the highest stage of union between the human intellect and the Active Intellect, one of the intelligences of the supernal world responsible for developing man's intellect from its original state of mere potentiality to a state of actuality. Ibn Daud nevertheless maintains the belief that prophecy is found only among the Jewish people and in the Holy Land.

To solve the problem of free will, ibn Daud discusses physics, metaphysics, and psychology. Ibn Daud moves furthest from Jewish philosophic tradition in his treatment of the problem of human free will and divine omniscience. The difficulty that confronted medieval philosophers was the apparent incompatibility of free will with the all-knowing power of God. Ibn Daud could only solve this difficulty by qualifying God's omniscience, maintaining that what is left to the free decision of man exists in a state of mere possibility until this decision has actually been made. He concluded that what is in essence merely possible must also be perceived by God as merely possible.

IN SUMMATION

Ibn Daud's *Sefer HaKabbalah* (*Book of Tradition*) had enormous influence down to modern times as an authority on the history of Spanish Jewry, and its comments on the Talmudic period in particular influenced the nineteenth-century Jewish historians. Although modern scholarship no longer accords it credence as objective history, it still remains a significant source for the life and thought of twelfth-century Spain.

Ibn Daud was also the first purely Aristotelian Jewish philosopher, and his works paved the way for others to follow. For the most part, though, his philosophy was only a lucid and systematic presentation of the main lines of Avicenna's basic teaching.

9

THE NEO-ARISTOTELIANISM OF MOSES MAIMONIDES

THE MAN AND HIS CULTURE

Moses Maimonides is considered to be the foremost intellectual figure in medieval Judaism. Commonly referred to as RaMBaM (an acronym for Rabbi Moses ben Maimon), he was born on March 30, 1135 in the city of Cordova on the Iberian Peninsula to the scholar and judge, Maimon ben Yoseph. His birth had such historical significance that the exact date and hour were recorded later by scholars of that period, and this was the sole known instance in which such was done in Jewish history.

The year 1148 has been known as a year of disaster in the history of the Jews in Spain in general and in the life of Maimonides in particular. In that year Almohades, a fanatic Moslem sect, under the leadership of Mahdi ibn Tumart captured Cordova, destroyed the Jewish community, and compelled the Christians and the Jews to convert to Islam or face exile. Maimonides and his family were among the exiles who traveled from one Spanish city to another, seeking refuge.

Realizing that the Talmud, the most authoritative rabbinic source of Judaism, was about to be neglected and forgotten as a result of the persecutions and because of the difficulty in its style and content, Maimonides began to compile his commentaries on a few of its tractates.

In 1159 he fled Spain and settled temporarily in Fez, Morocco. Several years later he resettled in Cairo, Egypt where scholars from all over the world turned to him on matters of religion and secular affairs.

In 1168 Maimonides completed his monumental work, the *Commentary on the Mishnah* to which he devoted ten years of his life. Immediately after completing his Mishnah commentaries, he began to codify and summarize the biblical and rabbinic law, religion, and ethics. He organized this teaching into a fourteen-volume work, which he called *Mishnah Torah* or *Yad Hazakaah*. This law code covered all phases of life including religion, holidays, women, business, human relations, hygiene, God, slavery, and scores of other subjects. A whole unit in the Code was devoted to education.

With the revival of the Greek sciences and philosophies in the Arab civilization of the Golden Era, contradictions were noted between the teachings of Aristotelian philosophy and the literal sense of the Bible. The Jewish scholars who were versed in biblical and rabbinic lore as well as in science and philosophy were perplexed. To guide the perplexed, Maimonides wrote in 1190 his philosophic treatise, *The Guide for the Perplexed (Moreh Nivuchim)*. This was his last major work of Jewish scholarship. Throughout his Guide, the position of Maimonides has been that of the classical exponent of rationalism in Jewish religious philosophy. He believed in the power of the human mind to grasp metaphysical truth. He further believed that metaphysics can only be apprehended by philosophic interpretations. Maimonides was among the first to base his philosophic interpretations of Judaism on the system of Aristotle. He thus preserved the basic principles of Judaism and upheld them against the extreme philosophic tendencies. It is important to note, however, that Maimonides closely followed the Aristotelian philosophy in all matters of science and logic, but not in matters of divinity. He believed that the theory of Aristotle is undoubtedly correct in all physical matters, but not in matters of theology. Maimonides' first philosophic topic is God. The following is a brief summary of his theology.

GOD IN MAIMONIDES' PRINCIPLES OF FAITH

Like Aristotle, Maimonides maintained that God exists, is a unity, and has no body. In Maimonides' *Commentary to the Mishnah*, he formulates his Thirteen Principles of Faith. His first principle is as follows: I believe with perfect faith that God is the Creator and ruler of all things. He alone has made, does make, and will make all things. In his commentary, Maimonides elaborates on this principle by maintaining that God is the Being, perfect in every possible way, who is the ultimate Cause of all existence. It is inconceivable that God does not exist, for if God did not exist, everything else would also cease to exist and nothing would remain. Only God is totally self-sufficient and, therefore, Unity and Mastery belong only to God. God is everything that He needs in Himself and does not need anything else at all. Everything else, however, whether it be an angel, a star, or anything associated with them above or below, all depend on Him for their very existence. Maimonides maintains that the Torah itself teaches this first principle of faith in the first of the Ten Commandments (Exodus 20:2): "I am the Lord your God."

His second principle states: I believe with perfect faith that God is One. There is no unity that is in any way like His. He alone is our God—He was, He is, and He will be. This principle involves the unity of God. God is not like any other single thinker, which can be divided into a number of elements. God is not even like the simplest physical thing, which is still infinitely divisible. Rather, God is One in a unique way. There is no other unity like His. The Torah itself teaches this second principle of faith when it says (Deuteronomy 6:4), "Hear O Israel, the Lord is our God, the Lord is One."

The third principle of faith of Maimonides states: I believe with perfect faith that God does not have a body. Physical concepts do not apply to Him. There is nothing whatsoever that resembles Him at all. This third principle maintains that God is totally incorporeal and that nothing associated with the physical can apply to God in any way. Thus, it cannot be said that God moves, rests, or exists in a given place. Things such as this can neither happen to Him, nor be part of His intrinsic nature. In answer to the question about places in the Bible where God is portrayed as walking, standing, speaking, and so forth, Maimonides emphatically posits that these are examples of the Bible speaking metaphorically and poetically. So, for example, when the Bible states that "God spoke," it is being used figuratively to mean that "God willed." The Torah itself teaches this third principle of faith when it says (Deuteronomy 4:15), "You have not seen any image." Thus it is impossible to conceive of God as having any image or form.

The fourth principle of faith of Maimonides states: I believe with perfect faith that God is first and last. The principle involves the absolute eternity of God. Nothing else shares God's eternal quality. This is discussed numerous times in the Bible, and the Torah teaches it when it says of God (Deuteronomy 33:27), "The eternal God is a refuge."

The fifth principle of faith states: I believe with perfect faith that it is only proper to pray to God. One may not pray to anyone or anything else. This principle teaches that God is the only one whom people may serve and praise. We may sing only of God's greatness and obey only His commandments. We may not act in this way toward anything beneath Him, whether it be an angel, a star, one of the elements, or any combination of them. All these have a predetermined nature and, therefore, none can have authority or free will. Only God has these attributes. It is therefore not proper to serve these things or make them intermediaries to bring us closer to God. All our thoughts should be directed only toward Him. Nothing else should even be considered. This fifth principle forbids all forms of idolatry, and it constitutes a major portion of the Torah.

The sixth principle of faith states: I believe with perfect faith that all the words of the prophets are true. This principle recognizes that there existed human beings, called prophets, to whom God communicated. These men and women had such lofty qualities and were able to achieve such great perfection that their souls became prepared to receive spiritual wisdom. Their human intellect could then become bound up with the Creative Mind and receive an inspired emanation from it. This is prophecy, and people who achieve it are the prophets.

The seventh principle of faith states: I believe with perfect faith that the prophecy of Moses is absolutely true. He was the chief of all prophets, both before and after him. This principle maintains that Moses, of all the prophets who ever lived, was able to attain the highest possible human level. He perceived the godly to a degree surpassing every human being who ever existed. He literally elevated himself from the level of the mere human to that of an angel.

Moses himself thus became like an angel. There was no barrier that he did not split and penetrate. Nothing physical held him back. He was not tainted by any deficiency, great or small. His thoughts, senses, and feelings ceased to exist entirely. His conscious mind was completely separated and became a pure spiritual thing. It is for this reason that he was able to speak to God without needing an angel as mediator and was therefore the greatest of the prophets.

The eighth principle of faith states: I believe with perfect faith that the entire Torah that we now have is that which was given to Moses. This principle maintains that Moses wrote the Torah down, much like a secretary taking dictation. Every word we have today was given directly to Moses by God.

Each verse in the Torah is equal in holiness. All the verses originate from God, and all are part of God's Torah, which is perfect, pure, holy, and true.

According to Maimonides, the person who asserts that some biblical passages were written by Moses of his own accord is considered by our prophets and sages to be the worst kind of nonbeliever, and a perverter of the Torah. Such a person claims that the Torah must be divided into a core and a shell, and that the stories and history contained in it were written by Moses and are of no true benefit.

The Torah itself teaches the fact that the entire Torah we now have was given to Moses when it says (Numbers 16:28), "Moses said, 'Through this you shall know that God sent me to do all these things, and I did not do it on my own accord.'"

The ninth principle of faith states: I believe with perfect faith that the Torah will not be changed, and that there will never be another Torah given by God. The principle involves permanence. That is to say, the Torah is God's permanent word, and no one else can change it. Nothing can be added to or subtracted from either the written Torah or the oral Torah. This is illustrated directly in the Torah when it states, "You shall not add to it, nor subtract from it" (Deuteronomy 13:1). According to Maimonides, if any prophet comes to alter the Torah, it is the clearest indicator that prophet is a false one. It does not matter whether he is Jewish or non-Jewish, or how many signs or miracles he performs. If he says that God sent him to add or subtract a commandment of the Torah or explains it differently than our tradition from Moses, he is a false prophet.

The tenth principle of faith states: I believe with perfect faith that God knows all of man's deeds and thoughts. This principle is taught by the Prophet Jeremiah when he says that God is "great in counsel, mighty in insight, whose eyes are open to all the ways of man" (Jeremiah 32:19). Another support text for this principle is Psalm 33:15: "God has molded every heart together and understands what each does." This principle essentially maintains that God knows all that people do, and He never turns His eyes away from them. However, Maimonides does maintain that people have absolute free will, and that God does not force them or decree upon them what to do.

The eleventh principle states: I believe with perfect faith that God rewards those who keep His commandments and punishes those who transgress His commandments. Maimonides posits that the greatest possible reward is the World to Come, while the greatest possible punishment is being cut off from it. The main reward for the righteous is in the World to Come. Here one can maintain a life that is not terminated by death and a good that is not mixed with any evil. The Torah itself teaches this principle in the following account. Moses said to God (Exodus 32:32), "If You will, then forgive their sin, but if not, then extinguish me." God answered (Exodus 32:33), "The one who has sinned against Me, him will I erase from My book." This shows that God knows both the obedient and the sinner, rewarding one and punishing the other.

The twelfth principle states: I believe with perfect faith in the coming of the Messiah. No matter how long it takes, I will await his coming every day. This principle maintains that the Messiah will certainly come and that people should not set a time for his coming or try to calculate when he will come based upon inferences from scriptural passages.

This principle also includes the belief that the Messiah will be greater than any other king or ruler who has ever lived. This, according to Maimonides, has been predicted by every prophet from Moses to Malachi. Also included in this principle is the belief that a Jewish king can only come from the family of David through his son Solomon. One who rejects this family denies God and His prophets.

The final and thirteenth principle of faith states: I believe with perfect faith that the dead will be brought back to life when God wills it to happen. The resurrection of the dead is one of the foundations handed down by Moses. Maimonides maintains that one who does not believe in it cannot be associated with Judaism.

The resurrection, however, is only for the righteous. This is based on the statement in the Talmud Taanit 7a, "Rain is for both the wicked and righteous, but the resurrection is only for the righteous." Maimonides comments on the absurdity for the wicked to be brought back to life, for even when they are alive, they are considered dead.

PROOFS OF THE EXISTENCE OF GOD

The second part of Maimonides' *Guide for the Perplexed* opens with the enumeration of the twenty-six propositions through which are proved the existence, unity, and incorporeality of God. Here are two of these proofs, the first for the unity of God, and the second for the existence of a Prime Mover.

Maimonides proves the unity of God by the following arguments:

1. Two gods cannot be assumed, for they would necessarily have one element in common by virtue of which they would be gods, and another element by which they would be distinguished from each other. Further, neither of them could have an independent existence, but both would themselves have to be created.

2. The whole existing world is "one" organic body, the parts of which are interdependent. The sublunary world is dependent upon the forces proceeding from the spheres, so that the whole universe is a macrocosm, and thus the effect must be due to one cause. The incorporeality of God can be proved by the preceding arguments and by the principle that every

corporeal object consists of matter and form, and that every compound requires an agent to effect its combination.

In a second proof (i.e., the existence of a Prime Mover), Maimonides offers the following reasoning. No motion can take place without an agent producing it, and the series of causes leading to a certain motion is finite. Since some things both receive and impart motion while other things are set in motion without imparting it, there must exist a being that imparts motion without being itself set in motion. As existing beings are partly permanent and partly transient, there must be a being whose existence is permanent. Nothing can pass from a state of potentiality into that of actuality without the intervention of an agent. This agent requires for its own transition from potentiality to actuality the help of another agent, and the latter, again, of another, and so on until one arrives at an agent that is constant and admits of no potentiality whatever.

MAIMONIDES' NEGATIVE THEOLOGY

In maintaining God's uniqueness, Maimonides states that the categories that are used to think about God must also be unique and unlike any others. It cannot, therefore, be assumed that the grammatical structures that apply to finite objects such as people also apply to God. Different subjects must be talked about in different ways. Correctly understood, a statement such as "God is powerful" tells us not what God is but what God is not. It says that God does not have any physical deficiencies. In this way Maimonides is able to turn all positive statements about God into negations, which separate the idea of God and therefore preserve its unique identity. In every case, Maimonides argues that God is radically unlike people, which is the crux of what has come to be termed "negative theology."

Thus, according to Maimonides, the only thing that people

can really say about God's nature is that it is off the scale of intelligibility. God is beyond all comprehension.

ORIGIN OF EVIL

Maimonides endeavors to show that evil has no positive existence but is a deprivation of a certain capacity and does not come from God. When evils are mentioned in the Bible as having been sent by God, Maimonides says that they must be explained allegorically. For him, all existing evils, with the exception of some which have their origin in the laws of production and destruction and which are rather an expression of God's mercy, are created by people themselves.

Finally, for Maimonides, evil is the denial of the good. It can be of the self-inflicted kind, as when people hurt and injure one another. Other forms of evil exist because the world is made out of material matter, which is subject to disintegration and decay.

PURPOSE OF THE DIVINE COMMANDMENTS

According to Maimonides, ethics and religion are linked together, and all the *mitzvot* aim either directly or indirectly at morality. Maimonides divides the commandments of the *Five Books of Moses* into fourteen groups and discusses the principal object of each group and the special object of each law. Thus, for example, the object of the laws concerning sacrifices lies in the accompanying prayers and devotions; as to the sacrifices themselves, they were only a concession to the idolatrous habits of the people.

In the opinion of Maimonides, the final aim of creation of this world is man, and man's final aim is that of happiness. This happiness consists of the exercise of man's intellect, which eventually leads to the cognition of truth. Maimonides asserts that the highest cognition is that of God and God's unity.

EDUCATIONAL PHILOSOPHY

Maimonides in his writings espoused a plethora of educational ideas. He devoted the entire sixth chapter in his book *Hilchot Deot* to a compendium of the virtues that characterize a scholar. The fifth chapter in his book *Hilchot Talmud Torah* outlined a code of conduct for students. Dr. Joshua Weinstein, a noted Professor of Education at the University of Houston, wrote a doctoral dissertation on Maimonides the educator. The following is a summary of his findings related to the educational philosophy of Maimonides.

Maimonides, like his predecessors, held the teacher in high regard. By virtue of his Aristotelian methodical approach, he superseded his mentors and systematically spelled out his opinions on the rights and obligations of the teachers. The teacher, by the right of his learning and scholarship, was regarded by Maimonides as a thorough aristocrat and was rendered honor and reverence. He based his ruling on the saying in the Mishnah, in Ethics of the Fathers: "the fear of your teacher shall be as the fear of Heaven." Since Maimonides also considered scholarly teachers to be the social elite, he insisted that they be the prototype of all that is refined, pious, and righteous. Modesty, good judgment, honesty, and patience were other major characteristics that made for good teaching.

Maimonides viewed learning as a process void of pragmatic objectives, and he considered the attainment of knowledge and truth as a purpose and a goal in itself. He considered the possession of wisdom to be the highest intellectual faculty of man. Recognizing the individual differences among human beings, Maimonides realized the need to employ different methods of motivation for different students. He recommended intrinsic motivations of learning for its own sake to those who had attained the highest level of mental maturity. For the masses, however, he prescribed extrinsic rewards of honor, wealth, and bliss in the hereafter.

Maimonides had a Gestalt outlook on the learning process and was interested in developing not only the intellectual faculties of the student but also his personality, attitude, manners, behavior—the whole student. He believed that just as a physician must know the body of his patient and his sickness before attempting treatment, so must he, who wishes to refine the soul, know its mental and psychological components.

Maimonides, the progressive liberal, who on many matters was found to think in the most advanced spirit of the twentieth century, proved to be an ultra conservative in the matter of education of women. His opinion coincided with that of his Greek mentors, Aristotle and Plato. Objecting to education of women, he reiterated an early saying of the sages that "He who teaches his daughter Torah—it is as if he taught her wantonness."

Regarding teaching techniques, Maimonides was a disciple of the ancient Greek thinkers. He recommended the employment of the Socratic questioning method in order to help stimulate the students' thinking. Maimonides did not confine the privilege of asking questions only to the teacher, but extended it to the students too. It stood to reason that he believed that this process of reciprocal challenge was to serve as an incentive to both the teacher and the students.

Maimonides was a forerunner of the idea of comprehensive and meaningful learning. He objected to drill and rote learning, and he emphasized the importance of the thinking process.

The following is a cross-section of the educational ideals of Maimonides as cited in the doctoral dissertation of Joshua Weinstein entitled "Maimonides the Educator":

1. Individual differences of students

2. Special education for the gifted

3. Limited size of the class

4. Employment of visual aids

5. The need for incentives to stimulate the learning process

6. The need for rapport between teacher and student

7. Maintenance of proper discipline to assure proper and constructive learning

8. The need for a testing program

IN SUMMATION

Maimonides, as a rationalist, was greatly influenced by Aristotle. He believed that God is One, incorporeal, eternal, and has given humankind an immutable Torah of instruction. He further maintained that God is unknowable and therefore everything written and said about God was done metaphorically in the language of the people so that they would be able to understand.

The greatest contribution of Maimonides in the field of education was the organization and systematic arrangement of educational principles. Many of Maimonides' ideas have been practiced through the last eight centuries and are practiced in many modern educational fields to this day.

In addition to its significance for medieval Jewish philosophy, Maimonides' works also have had a formative influence on modern Jewish thought. He provided a first acquaintance with philosophic speculation for a number of philosophers of the Enlightenment period and served as a bridge for the study of modern philosophy.

Maimonides was also one of the few Jewish thinkers whose teachings also influenced the non-Jewish world. Thomas Aquinas, for example, refers in his writings to "Rabbi Moses" and shows considerable familiarity with his writing.

In 1985, on the eight hundred fiftieth anniversary of Maimonides' birth, a UNESCO conference on Maimonides was held in Paris. At this conference, Shlomo Pines was quoted as saying, "Maimonides is the most influential Jewish thinker of the Middle Ages, and quite possibly of all time" (*Time*, December 23, 1985).

10

MOSES BEN NACHMAN (NACHMONIDES)

BACKGROUND

Moses ben Nachman, also known as Nachmonides and RaM-BaN, was a Spanish rabbi, philosopher, and biblical commentator. Born in Gernon, Catalonia in 1194, he was a descendant of Isaac ben Reuben. He exercised extensive influence over Jewish public life in Catalonia. Even King James I was known to consult him.

One of the most famous Jewish-Christian disputes was between the apostate Jew Pablo Christiani and Nachmonides. In the debate, Nachmonides argued that the central issue separating Christianity and Judaism was not the issue of Jesus as the messiah, but whether or not Jesus was divine. Nachmonides argued that Jews do not believe that Jesus was the messiah because he did not fulfill the biblical messianic prophecies. At the request of the bishop of Gerona, Nachmonides summarized his views in a book entitled *Sefer haVikuach*. Following the debate, Nachmonides left Spain and emigrated to Palestine. In

Jerusalem he organized the remnants of the Jewish community, erected a synagogue, and founded a yeshivah.

About fifty works by Nachmonides have been preserved. The majority of them are novellas on the Talmud and Jewish law. He wrote a work entitled *Sefer HaGe'ullah* that describes belief in redemption. He was also a gifted liturgical poet, writing a number of poems and prayers. Several of his sermons have also been preserved, including "HaDerashah laChatunah" and "Torat Hashem Temimah."

In 1268 Nachmonides moved to Acre where he became the spiritual leader of the Jewish community. He died in approximately 1270. It is conjectured that he may have been buried at the foot of Mount Carmel, in Acre, or possibly even in Jerusalem.

BIBLICAL COMMENTARY AND PHILOSOPHY

Nachmonides wrote most of his biblical commentary later on in life. Unlike his most noted predecessors Rashi and Abraham ibn Ezra whose commentaries dealt with explanations of individual words and verses, Nachmonides concerns himself more with the sequence of biblical passages and the deeper meaning of the Bible's laws and narrative. He makes frequent use of both legendary and legal interpretations of the talmudic and midrashic sages. Nachmonides spends a great deal of time critically analyzing them and their ideas.

Nachmonides' biblical commentary clearly reflects his views on God, the Torah, Israel, and the world. The Torah is the word of God and is the source of all knowledge. The biblical narratives are not only records of the past but portents of the future.

The account of the six days of creation contains prophecies regarding the most important events of the succeeding six thousand years, while the Sabbath foreshadows the seventh millennium, which will be the Day of the Lord.

Regarding the *mitzvot*, Nachmonides maintains that there is a reason for every one of them. The commandments are all for the good of man, either to keep man from something hurtful, to remove man from evil habits, or to teach mercy and goodness.

In his commentary on the Book of Job, Nachmonides suggests that the answer to the problem of the suffering of the righteous and the prosperity of the wicked—the central theme of the book—is to be found in the belief of transmigration of souls. The righteous are punished and the wicked rewarded for their deeds in an earlier life.

NACHMONIDES AS HALAKHIST

Nachmonides' legal works can be divided into the following categories: novellas on the Talmud, Halakhic monographs, *hassagot* (i.e., criticisms), and Responsa.

His novellas, which originally covered the entire Talmudic orders of Moed, Nashim, and Nezikin, are based on the best of the earlier Spanish tradition. He constantly availed himself of the writings of Shmuel HaNagid, Isaac Alfasi, and Joseph ibn Migash. He inaugurated a new school in the method of studying the Oral Law, which laid the emphasis on an apprehension, for its own sake, of the Talmudic *sugya* (theme) as a whole, in point both of its inner tenor and of its relation to other relevant themes throughout the Talmud.

In his works he was also constantly searching for ancient, critically examined, and established Talmudic texts so as not to become involved in needless discussions to solve questions arising from difficult readings. Nachmonides also made extensive use of the Geonic writings and the Jerusalem Talmud. His novellas are notable for their wealth of sources and clear, logical mode of presentation. He also devotes much space to methodological discussions on the principles of the Talmud.

The second class of Nachmonides' Halakhic literary works comprises his seven monographs:

1. Dinei de Garme deals with a clarification of the laws regarding inconvenience to a neighbor and injury to his property.

2. Mishpetay haCherem deals with the way in which a ban is imposed and release obtained from it.

3.–5. Hilchot Bechorot and Hilchot Challah deal with the laws of firstborns and the separation of *Challah*.

6. Torat HaAdam deals with the laws of death and mourning and those concerning visiting the sick.

7. Hilchot Niddah deals with the laws of ritual impurity.

The third category of Nachmonides' Halakhic writings comprises his works of criticism, of which there are three: (1) *hassagot* ("criticisms") of Maimonides' *Sefer Ha Mitzvot*; (2) Milchamot Adonai, attacking Zerahiah haLevi's criticisms of Hilchot haRif; and (3) *Sefer HaZechut*, attacking Abraham ben David's criticism of Alfasi.

Nachmonides' Halakhic writings had a decisive influence on the entire history of subsequent rabbinic literature.

IN SUMMATION

Nachmonides has left us with a rich Bible commentary with its characteristic combination of rational interpretation (often with contemporary allusions) and insistence on kabbalistic implications. His glosses on the Talmud, similar to, though more practical than, those of the French tosaphists, established his reputation as the foremost Spanish Talmudist. His legal writings had an important influence on the entire history of subsequent rabbinic literature.

From the time his novellas first appeared in print, their influence has become increasingly pronounced, especially among Ashkenazi students and yeshivot. To this day their study occupies in the yeshivot of Polish-Lithuanian origin a principal place together with Rashi, the tosafot, and Maimonides.

11

LEVI BEN GERSHOM

BACKGROUND

Levi ben Gershom (RaLBaG), commonly known as Gersonides, was a French philosopher and exegete. He lived primarily in Orange in the first half of the fourteenth century and briefly at Avignon. Relatively little is known of his life beyond the fact that he maintained relations with some important Christians of his day. His scientific works deal with arithmetic, geometry, trigonometry, and astronomy. He was also a noted Talmudist and liturgist. He never held a rabbinic office, probably earning his living by the practice of medicine.

BIBLICAL COMMENTARIES

Levi ben Gershom wrote commentaries on Job (1325), Song of Songs (1325), Ecclesiastes (1328), Ruth (1329), Esther (1329), the *Five Books of Moses* (1329 to 1338), the Former Prophets (1338), Proverbs, Daniel, Nehemiah, and Chronicles (1338).

His biblical commentaries are the work of an exegete and a philosopher. He discusses an array of both philosophic and theological issues in his commentaries, including the topics of providence, miracles, and the Messiah. From each biblical book he extracts the ethical, philosophic, and religious teachings, calling them *to'aliyyot*. A collection of these teachings was printed separately in 1570. In his lengthy commentary on the *Five Books of Moses*, Levi ben Gershom sets out to reconstitute the *Halacha* (Jewish law) rationally, basing himself on nine principles of logic. He totally condemns allegorical interpretations.

PHILOSOPHY

Levi's major work is entitled *Milchamot Adonai* (*Wars of the Lord*) in six books. Its main themes are as follows: (1) the immortality of the soul, which depends on each person's degree of philosophic knowledge or contact with the Active Intellect; (2) Divination and Prophecy, with Prophecy being the highest degree of contact with the Active Intellect; (3) Divine Omnipotence; (4) Divine Providence, which extends over species and general matters, not over individuals, since God cannot know the particular; (5) Astronomy; (6) Creation and Miracles. God created the world from formless primal matter, and miracles are caused by the Active Intellect.

Demonstrating the existence of God, Levi rejects the proof (favored by many of his Aristotelian predecessors) of God as a prime mover. In its place Levi presents a proof based upon the orderly processes existing in the world. According to this proof of design, the observed regularity of processes of generation within the world leads to the conclusion that these processes are produced by an intelligence. This intelligence endows matter with its various forms. For Levi ben Gershom, the orderliness of both the celestial and terrestrial worlds points to a supreme being that produces the order. This supreme being is God.

Unlike Maimonides who holds to the doctrine of negative theology, Levi maintains that it is possible to ascribe positive attributes to God without damaging God's unity. Levi teaches that man may have a certain positive knowledge of God, based on the observation of His actions. The essential action of God is thinking, and consequently the dispensation of all forms. All the attributes that man recognizes in his own are just so many attributes of God.

Man is given personal freedom, and any individual who makes use of his or her freedom is no longer subject to the universal law known by God. For Levi, God's knowledge embraces all the world's events, with the exception of free acts that cannot be predicted by any type of knowledge. In this way Levi ben Gershom has succeeded in reconciling two contradictory fundamental principles of the Bible: God as all-knowing and the freedom of a person's will.

GOD'S OMNISCIENCE

The third part of Levi's *Milchamot* deals with God's omniscience. Aristotle argued that God's knowledge was limited to universal only, asserting that if God had knowledge of particulars, He would be subject to constant changes. In rejecting Aristotle's view, Maimonides argued that belief in an all-knowing God is not in opposition to belief in God's unity. Maimonides believed that God was able to perceive future events before they occurred.

Levi ben Gershom argues that there can be no doubt that there is a wide degree of difference between human knowledge and God's knowledge. Levi refutes Maimonides' view of God's omniscience, arguing that the exalted thought of God embraces all the cosmic laws that regulate the evolution of nature, the general influences exercised by the celestial bodies on the sublunary world, and the specific essences with which matter is invested. But sublunary events, the multifaceted details of the phenomenal world, are hidden from God's spirit. Not to know these details is not imperfection, since in knowing the universal conditions of things, God knows that which is essential, and consequently good, in the individual.

GOD'S PROVIDENCE

The providence is discussed in the fourth division of Levi's book *Milchamot*. Aristotle's theory that humanity only as a whole is guided by a divine providence admits the existence of neither prophecy nor divination. Levi ben Gershom asserts that the providence of God extends a means of protection that increases in proportion to man's moral and intellectual perfections. Through the determined activities of the stars, God assures a maximum of good to men in general and spares them a maximum of ills. Portents, dreams, prophecies, and the exercise of free choice save certain individuals from harmful effects of determinism. However, for Levi ben Gershom, the existence of evil cannot be denied, since at times the righteous do suffer. But Levi upholds the belief that the true good, which is specifically human, is the immortality of the soul, and it is this immortality, proportioned according to one's moral integrity, that constitutes the actual recompense of God.

CREATION OF THE WORLD AND MIRACLES

The last division of Levi ben Gershom's *Milchamot* deals with creation and with miracles. After having refuted the arguments advanced by Aristotle in favor of the eternity of the world and having proved that neither time nor motion is infinite, Levi demonstrates that the world had a beginning, that it has no end, and that the world did not proceed from another world. In opposition to Maimonides who held that the creation of the world cannot be demonstrated philosophically, Levi ben Gershom offers philosophic arguments designed to show that the world came into being. One such argument is that everything produced by a final cause, ordained to a certain end, cannot exist eternally. Since the world fulfills all these conditions, it follows that it cannot be eternal, but rather has a beginning in time.

Regarding the actual creation of the world, Levi ben Gershom posits a middle position between the theory of the existence of a primordial cosmic substance and that of a creation *ex nihilo*. According to him, there existed from eternity inert undetermined matter, devoid of form and attribute. At a given moment God bestowed upon this matter essence, form, and motion. From it proceeded all sublunary being and all heavenly substances, with the exception of the separated intelligences, which were direct emanations of the Divinity.

In the second part of the last division of his work, Levi ben Gershom endeavors to demonstrate that his theory of creation agrees with the account of the Book of Genesis. He further demonstrates that the actual performer of miracles is neither God nor prophet, but the active intellect. There are, he writes, two kinds of natural laws: those regulating the economy of the heavens and those that govern the special operations of the demiurgic principle and by which are produced extraordinary phenomena known as miracles. Like freedom in the will in man, this faculty was given by God to the active intellect as a corrective of the influences of the celestial bodies. Thus a person of a highly developed intellect may foresee the accomplishment of a certain miracle that is only the result of a providential law conceived and executed by the active intellect.

According to Levi, miracles are subjected to several laws: their effect cannot remain permanently and supersede the law of nature; no miracle can produce self-contradictory things (e.g., an object that can be black and white at the same time); and no miracle can take place in the celestial spheres. Thus, when

Joshua said (Joshua 10:12), "Sun, stand still upon Gibeon," Levi asserts that he was merely expressing the desire that the defeat of the enemy should be completed while the sun continued to shine.

ESCHATOLOGY

Levi ben Gershom's eschatology is based on a tradition that there are two Messiahs. After the Messiah son of Joseph dies, having been assassinated, the Messiah son of David will appear. According to Levi, he will be greater than Moses, not because he will teach a new Torah, but because he will accomplish a miracle greater than those of Moses: the resurrection of the dead, an event that will convert all peoples of the earth to the true religion. Levi predicted the coming of the Messiah for the year 1358.

IN SUMMATION

Levi ben Gershom's philosophic theories, some of which influenced Spinoza, met with great opposition among the Jews. While Crescas criticized them on philosophic grounds, others attacked them merely because they were not in keeping with the ideas of orthodoxy. Some zealous rabbis went so far as to prohibit the study of Levi ben Gershom's Bible commentaries.

However, even the most vocal critics of Levi did not hesitate to borrow or adapt some of his ideas, and his influence continued to exert itself even as late as the nineteenth century, when he is mentioned in the commentator Malbim's commentary on the Book of Job. Indeed, Levi ben Gershom was an impassioned rationalist in the medieval Jewish tradition who was more willing to accept the implications of this basic Aristotelian system than any of his medieval colleagues.

12

CRITICS OF ARISTOTELIANISM: HASDAI CRESCAS

BACKGROUND

This religious philosopher was born in Spain in 1340. A student of the well-known Talmudist Nissim ben Reuben (RaN), he became a Talmudic authority and philosopher. With the accession of John I in 1387, Crescas became closely associated with the court of Aragon.

Toward the end of the fourteenth century, Crescas was actively involved in the general rehabilitation of Spanish Jewry. He also made efforts to reform the system of communal representation in Saragossa.

Crescas did not have a great deal of time for writing. What he did write was motivated by his desire to rescue Judaism in Spain. As part of a campaign to combat the vast array of Christianizing literature aimed at Jews and Conversos, he wrote his "Refutation of the Principles of the Christians." This work is basically a critique of ten principles of Christianity: original sin, redemption, the Trinity, the incarnation, the virgin birth, transubstantiation, baptism, Jesus as the messiah, the New Testament, and demonology. Even his philosophic treatise *Or Adonai* (*Light of God*), an anti-Aristotelian classic, was a polemic against Christianity. Another work, *Ner Mitzvah* (*Lamp of Mitzvah*), was intended to have superseded Maimonides' Halakhic work *Mishnah Torah*. It was never written.

The last decade of Crescas' life was devoted exclusively to his literary activities. He died at Saragossa.

OR ADONAI

In his preface to this volume, Crescas argued that it is absurd to speak of a divine commandment to believe in the existence of God, since such a belief cannot be a commandment itself, but rather a presupposition for any commandment. Before one can speak of a divine commandment, one must already be convinced of the existence of a divine commander, namely God. Crescas asserted that belief is involuntary, and one can only be reasonably commanded to do what one has the power to choose to do. Thus, belief in the existence of God is a presupposition of all the commandments, but it itself is not a commandment.

Or Adonai is divided into four books that analyze the following: (1) the presuppositions of Torah; (2) the fundamentals of Torah; (3) other obligatory beliefs of Torah; and (4) some nonobligatory speculations. Following Maimonides, Crescas considers as presuppositions God's existence, unity, and incorporeality. His analysis is tripartite: (1) a thorough presentation of the alleged Aristotelian presuppositions of Torah; (2) a disproof of Aristotelianism; and (3) a new investigation of the presuppositions.

Crescas refutes the Aristotelian arguments against the existence of a vacuum and suggests that a medium is not a necessary condition of either motion or weight. This allows him to argue against the impossibility of infinite incorporeal and corporeal magnitudes and in the process to overthrow Aristotle's definition of place.

Crescas also rejects the Aristotelian view that the celestial spheres possess intelligence and that their motion is voluntary. He argues that motion of both terrestrial as well as celestial elements is natural rather than rational. Crescas also rejects Aristotle's definition of time as an accident of motion.

The critique of the Aristotelian propositions was also the critique of the premises of Maimonides' proofs of the existence, unity, and incorporeality of God. And the proofs fall within the propositions. Crescas does, however, recognize one short proof of the existence of God. Regardless of whether causes and effects in the world are finite or infinite, there must be one cause of all of them as a whole. For were there nothing but effects, these effects in themselves would have only possible existence. Hence, in order to bring them into actual being, they need a cause, and this cause is God.

For Crescas, Torah is the product of a voluntary action from the Commander, who is both the initiator of the action to the commanded and the receiver of the action. Fundaments are concepts that necessarily follow from his conception of Torah. They include: (1) God's knowledge of existents, for God could not have commanded the Torah without knowing what he commanded; (2) providence, for God's voluntary giving of the Torah was itself providential (according to Crescas, God provides for individuals not, as Maimonides taught, in accordance with their intellectual excellence, but on the merit of their love); (3) God's powers, for were God powerless, He could not have given the Torah (Crescas argued that God who created all by virtue of His will is infinitely powerful, and not dependent upon nature); (4) communication between Commander and commanded (i.e., prophecy, for the Torah is the product of such communication) and Crescas maintains that prophecy is not the culmination of philosophy, as Maimonides asserts, but of love for God; (5) man's power of choice, for the concept of commandment presupposes the commanded's ability to choose to obey (Crescas accepts the theological position of determinism, which holds that God foresees all, yet freedom of choice is given to man); and (6) the purposefulness of Torah, which includes the idea that the Torah, produced by the Prime Intellect (God), must have a purpose. This purpose includes love of man and the correction of man's opinions.

PHILOSOPHY

Against both Platonism and Aristotelianism, Crescas argues that God's love for man is stronger than man's love for God, for God's infinite essence is the source of both loves. For Crescas, man's love for God results in *devekut* (communion with God).

Of the nonfundamental obligatory beliefs, Crescas distinguishes those independent of specific commandments, which include creation, survival of the soul, reward and punishment, resurrection, immutability of the Torah, the distinction between Moses and the other prophets, and the Messiah. Those dependent upon specific commandments include the efficacy of prayer, God's readiness to accept the penitent, and the spiritual value of the High Holy Days.

GOD, SOUL, AND THE MESSIAH

What is crucial for Crescas is that the world is created *ex nihilo* by the absolute will of God, and that only the existence of God is necessary. Creation need not be in time, for God is creating each day. Differing from Maimonides who only speaks of God's negative attributes, Crescas writes of God's positive attributes (e.g., eternity, knowledge), terms which are employed amphibolously. Their generic meaning is the same when they are applied to God as when they are applied to human beings. However, human attributes are finite whereas God's attributes are infinite. For Crescas, God is Goodness, and God's happiness is in His infinite creation of good and infinite love for His creatures.

In his discussion of the soul, Crescas rejects the Aristotelian theory that only the acquired intellect survives death. He argues that the soul is a simple and incorruptible substance, whose essence is not the intellect but something sublime.

Concerning the Messiah, Crescas posits that he will be greater than both Moses and the angels.

IN SUMMATION

Although Crescas' *Or Adonai* was written for philosophers, there is no doubt that he was influenced by mystical kabbalists. He cites several mystical books, including *Sefer Yetzirah* and *Sefer HaBahir*, and he often interprets the Bible kabbalistically. Giordano Bruno, the sixteenth-century Christian Italian philosopher, has borrowed from him, and Spinoza's theories of extension, freedom, and love are marked by his close study of *Or Adonai*.

13

JOSEPH ALBO

BACKGROUND

Joseph Albo was a Spanish preacher and philosopher of the fifteenth century, known chiefly as the author of the work on the fundamentals of Judaism called *Sefer Halkkarim (Book of Principles)*. Little is known of the details of his life. Montreal, a town in Aragon, is generally assumed to have been his birthplace. Astruc, in his report of the prolonged religious debate held at Tortosa in 1413 to 1414, mentions Albo as one of the Jewish participants.

Albo's use of medical illustrations creates the presumption that he was adept in medical science, thus emulating the excellent tradition of earlier Jewish writers on philosophic subjects. One of Albo's noteworthy teachers was Hasdai Crescas, an important Spanish philosopher and statesman.

BOOK OF PRINCIPLES

Albo's *Book of Principles* is one of the representative books of the period in which he lived. It reflects his worried reaction to the wavering of faith among his fellow Jews that stemmed from the discussions of religious dogma. Albo felt the need to restore the morale of his people by offering them a reasoned presentation of Judaism and by showing that the fundamental teachings of the Jewish religion bore the essential character of a "divine law." He brought to his work knowledge of both rabbinic literature and Jewish philosophy.

Basic to Albo's investigation is the recognition that human happiness is conditioned by knowledge and conduct. However, human intellect cannot attain perfect knowledge and ethical conduct because its power is limited. Therefore, there must be something above human intellect through which knowledge and conduct can attain to a degree of excellence that admits of no doubt. According to Albo, the insufficiency of human intellect postulates the necessity of divine guidance, and thus it is the duty of man to know the God-given law. But in order to know it, one must have established the true principles, without which there can be no divine law. Albo attempts to create a structure for the true religion by establishing fundamental principles. He does this by attempting to answer the question, What principles are indispensable to a religion that is both divine and true? One of Albo's intended purposes in writing his *Book of Principles* was not to place Judaism upon a solid philosophic foundation, but to vindicate for Judaism, as opposed to the other revealed religions, the right to the distinction of being the true revealed religion.

Albo's terminology is probably original with him. The three fundamentals he designates as *ikkarim*—principles. Hence the title of the book: the *Book of Principles*. The eight derived and necessary truths form the indispensable elements of the Divine Law. Albo calls these truths *shorashim*, or roots.

In his writings Albo finds time to criticize the opinions of his predecessors. He rejects the assumption that creation out of nothing is an essential implication of the belief in God. He is critical of the articles of faith of Maimonides, and also of the six that Crescas had evolved.

According to Albo, the first of his fundamental root principles (the belief in the existence of God) embraces the following principles: (1) God's unity; (2) God's incorporeality; (3) God's independence of time; and (4) God's perfection.

The second root principle, the belief in revelation, or the communication of divine instruction by God to man, leads him to derive the following three secondary radicals: (1) the appointment of prophets as the mediums of this divine revelation; (2) the belief in the unique greatness of Moses as a prophet; and (3) the binding force of the Mosaic law until another shall have been proclaimed in as public a manner (before six hundred thousand people). No later prophet has, consequently, the right to abrogate the Mosaic dispensation.

According to Albo, the belief in the Messiah is only a twig or a branch. It is quite likely that the relegation of the belief in a Messiah to a rank below that of a principle was designed to refute Christian teaching, which made this belief so central to its dogma. Albo even went further to say that should it be proven that the Messiah had already come, he would not consider himself less faithful a Jew. It is not necessary to the soundness of the trunk, and not an integral part of Judaism. Nor is it true that every law is binding.

ALBO'S CONCEPT OF DIVINE LAW

The concept of Divine Law, which is crucial for Albo, is introduced by him in the context of the discussion of the three kinds of law, namely, natural law, conventional law, and Divine law. This scheme was taken over from Thomas Aquinas.

For Albo, the superiority of the Divine Law over natural and conventional law derives from its purpose, which is to guide people to the attainment of true felicity, namely, the felicity of the soul and immortality. Whereas natural law aims at ordering human society and conventional law seeks to improve the social order, the Divine Law embraces both the realm of *middot* (conduct) and *de'ot* (beliefs). It is therefore, in the words of Psalm 19:8, "perfect, restoring the soul." Albo uses Psalm 19 to demonstrate the superiority of the Divine Law over the conventional and natural laws.

IN SUMMATION

Albo's doctrine of derived principles had great significance, offering a criterion of truth of those faiths that claimed to be divinely revealed. He posited the possibility of a plurality of revealed religions and developed the idea that the difference between the laws of the various religions was grounded in the variant natures of the people for whom they were established and to which they are appropriate. Refusing though to recognize extrabiblical faiths, Albo always maintained the exclusive character of the biblical revelation.

Albo also rejected the philosophic doctrine that one could attain bliss through the perfection of the intellect. It was not knowledge, but rather the observance of divine precepts, which was required. If a person observed the precepts with the proper intention, they operated on that person's soul in order to prepare it for everlasting life.

By basing Judaism on general religious principles, Albo's system has considerable significance as an apologetic, particularly anti-Christian theology. Although Albo's originality has been questioned, his works achieved great popularity in Jewish circles among both laypersons and scholars. S. Back, in his dissertation on Joseph Albo (Breslau, 1869), places him on a high pedestal as the first Jewish thinker who had the courage to coordinate philosophy and religion, or even to make both identical.

14

ISAAC ABRABANEL

BACKGROUND

One of the oldest and most distinguished Spanish families was that of the Abrabanel family, which traces its origin from King David. Isaac Abrabanel, son of the Portuguese treasurer Dom Judah, was born in 1437 in Lisbon and died in Venice in 1508. A student of Joseph Chayim, rabbi of Lisbon, Abrabanel was well versed in Talmudic literature, devoting his early years to the study of Jewish religious philosophy. At age twenty he wrote on the original form of the natural elements and on a variety of religious questions. He entered the service of King Alfonso V of Portugal, serving as his treasurer. After the death of Alfonso, he was obliged to relinquish his office, having been accused by King John II of connivance with the Duke of Braganca, who had been executed on the charge of conspiracy. He fled to Castile in 1483 and made Toledo his new home. There, he occupied himself at first with biblical studies, producing an extensive commentary on the Books of Joshua, Judges, and Samuel.

His final years were spent in Naples where in 1493 he completed his commentary on the Book of Kings. In 1503 he settled in Venice, finishing commentaries on the Book of Jeremiah, the minor prophets, Genesis, Exodus, Leviticus, and Numbers. It was in Venice that he died.

ABRABANEL AS AUTHOR AND COMMENTATOR

Abrabanel's works may be divided into three classes, referring to: (1) exegesis, such as his commentary upon the Bible; (2) philosophy, dealing with both general philosophy and philosophy of the Jewish religion; and (3) apologetics, in defense of the Jewish doctrine of the Messiah.

Regarding his commentaries, Abrabanel held that it was not sufficient to consider only the literary elements of the Bible. Rather, it was imperative to also take into account the political and social life of the people. As such, he prefaced each of his biblical books of commentary with a general introduction concerning the character of each book, its date of composition, and the author's intention. For this reason he was considered a pioneer of the modern science of biblical propaedeutics. Christian scholars of the seventeenth and eighteenth centuries used and studied Abrabanel's many commentaries. Interestingly, Abrabanel closely studied many Christian commentaries, such as Jerome and Augustine, showing extreme tolerance toward them and their works. On the other hand, he strongly denounced Jewish philosophers such as Albalag and Gersonides for their liberal standpoint that they assumed regarding religio-philosophic questions.

ABRABANEL AS CRITICAL BIBLICAL INTERPRETER

Abrabanel's commentaries are largely influenced by earlier interpreters such as Isaac Arama and Levi ben Gershom. Like the latter, he divided the books into his own chapters, each containing an introduction in which he sets forth the difficulties about to be encountered in the chapter. The questions he identifies at times number more than forty, while in his commentary on the Prophets he limits himself to six questions. Grammatical or philological explanations of the biblical are not usually given in his commentaries. In this area, Abrabanel is more likely to rely on those of his predecessors, in particular David Kimchi.

Each chapter is prefaced by a brief resume of its content, followed by a lengthy excursus of the subject matter in which he tries to resolve those problems raised in the introduction.

Some of Abrabanel's interpretations derive from sermons delivered in the synagogue. He vigorously fought the extreme rationalism of philosophic interpretation as well as interpretations based on philosophic allegory. Although he avoided mystical interpretations, he nevertheless believed that the Torah did have its share of hidden meanings and thus he interpreted Bible passages in various ways, including the presentation of the moral lessons derived from the text. He also quoted extensively from the Midrash.

ABRABANEL AS PHILOSOPHER

The religious philosophy of Abrabanel appears throughout his many works, and not in any single volume. Although Abrabanel is often considered the last Jewish Aristotelian, he was essentially an opponent of philosophy, for his entire understanding of philosophy, in opposition to Maimonides and his school, was rooted in the conviction of God's revelation in history, and particularly in the history of the selected people.

Critics have asserted that many of Abrabanel's views were confused, being both Maimonistic and anti-Maimonistic at the same time, while also to some measure being kabbalistic. An example of his wavering is afforded by his religious work entitled "Rosh Emunah" (Pinnacle of Faith), based on Song of

Songs 4:8. This work, devoted to the championship of Maimonides' thirteen principles of faith against the attacks of Joseph Albo, concludes with the statement that Maimonides gathered these articles merely in accordance with the fashion of other nations, which set up fundamental principles for their science. But the Jewish religion, he asserted, has nothing in common with human science; the teachings of the Torah are revelations from God, making them all equal in value; and among them are neither principles nor corollaries from these principles. Certainly these conclusions are unusual for a work that purports to be a defense of Maimonides.

It appears that when Abrabanel thinks that Maimonides in his writing deviates from traditional belief, he vigorously criticizes him. For example, he attacks Maimonides' conception that the visions of the prophets were the creations of imagination. For Abrabanel, even the so-called *Bat Kol* (Divine Voice) of the Talmud was an authentic voice made audible by God. This miracle he describes in his commentary on Genesis, chapter 16. Furthermore, whereas Maimonides notes that the prophecy of Moses was superior in nature to that of other prophets, Abrabanel reaffirms the essential similarity between Moses' prophecy and that of the other prophets. Abrabanel's theory of prophecy is essentially the rabbinic one. All prophecy is produced miraculously by God, and every prophetic vision is real and qualitatively superior to scientific knowledge.

ABRABANEL AS APOLOGETE

One point of Maimonides' system which Abrabanel defended and imitated was that of a belief in a Messiah. Abrabanel felt the despair of the Jewish people who were expelled from Spain, and therefore set himself to champion the cause of the Messiah as the way to bring hope and peace to the world.

With this goal, he wrote the following three works: "Mayene haYeshuah" (Sources of Salvation), "Yeshu'ot Meshicho" (Salvation of His Anointed), and "Mashmiah Yeshu'a" (Proclaiming Salvation). All of these were completed in the years 1497 to 1498. Each work was devoted to a discourse related to the Messiah and the messianic era.

"Mayene haYeshuah" is a commentary on the biblical book of Daniel, in which he disputes both the Christian exposition and the Jewish rationalism of the book. Quite peculiar is the fact that Abrabanel counts Daniel among the prophets, unlike in rabbinic tradition, coinciding therein with the current Christian interpretation. The remainder of his commentary is devoted to an exhaustive criticism of the Christian exposition.

Abrabanel's second work, "Yeshu'ot Meshicho," is an exposition of the doctrine concerning the Messiah according to the traditional testimony of the Talmud and Midrash.

In his third apologetic work, Abrabanel collects biblical messianic passages of the Bible and their interpretations. Throughout this volume, Abrabanel constantly attacks the Christian interpretation of these passages.

ABRABANEL'S UNDERSTANDING OF HISTORY

Abrabanel bases his understanding of history on the Bible, the source of truth. The Bible provides both the history of the universe and the history of man. The foundation is the personal God who creates the universe *ex nihilo* (i.e., out of nothing). Thus for Abrabanel, the universe presents no pre-existent nature that has the capability of limiting God's powers. God is in control of nature, and thus Abrabanel rejects the naturalism of Maimonides. What befalls people is directly attributable to God, human freedom, or supernatural beings. This is the significance of Abrabanel's system of angelology and demonology. In naturalistic Judaism, the biblical angels have been reduced to natural forces. For Abrabanel, natural forces are reduced to angels and demons who always fulfill the will of God.

Abrabanel's view of history is essentially the rabbinic one. God created the universe according to a grandiose design that culminates in the salvation of people. God exercised a special destiny for the Jewish people, revealing to them His will through the Torah and giving them the Land of Israel. The Land of Israel is most well suited for spiritual growth and the reception of prophecy.

ESCHATOLOGY

One of Abrabanel's great achievements was his defense of the rabbinic concept of salvation against the Christian claim that Jesus was the Messiah. Both Christian and Jewish exegesis drew on the Bible as evidence for the Messiah. Abrabanel gave strong support for the Jewish view. In his interpretation of the eschatological Book of Daniel, Abrabanel's interpretation included his prediction that the messianic age would arrive in the year 1503. At that time the Jews would defeat their enemies, return to the Land of Israel, and the Messiah's rule would extend over all people. This would allow for a mankind to emerge that would be capable of realizing its full spiritual potential. It has been said that the speculation of Abrabanel in this area contributed in part to the many messianic movements of the sixteenth and seventeenth centuries.

IN SUMMATION

Abrabanel was the last Jewish Aristotelian. Of particular noteworthiness is his exegesis, characterized in the Encyclopedia Judaica, volume 2, page 106, by three innovations:

1. His comparison of the social structure of society in biblical times with that of the European society in his day (for example, in dealing with the institution of monarchy, 1 Samuel 8). He had wide recourse to historical interpretation, particularly in his commentaries to the Major and Minor Prophets and to the Book of Daniel, but in numerous instances his interpretations are anachronistic (for example, Judges 18).

2. Preoccupation with Christian exegesis and exegetes. He generally disputed their christological interpretations, especially those of Jerome. But he did not hesitate to borrow from them when their interpretations seemed correct to him.

3. His introductions to the books of the prophets, which are much more comprehensive than those of his predecessors. In them he deals with the content of the books, the division of the material, their authors, and the time of compilation, and he also draws comparisons between the method and style of the various prophets.

Some of his commentaries have been translated into Latin and have influenced biblical research in humanistic circles.

15

MYSTICISM AND ISAAC LURIA

BACKGROUND

Jewish mysticism, or *kabbalah* as it is known in Hebrew, is the form of Jewish religion that, through its esoteric teachings, seeks to cultivate personal communion between the worshiper and God. One of the distinguishing marks of Jewish mysticism is the intensity of religious feeling, rising frequently from ecstasy, which gives to it a dynamic force unknown to the ordinary religion.

Like other kinds of mysticism, *kabbalah* draws upon the mystic's awareness of both the transcendence and immanence of God within the true religious life, every facet of which is a revelation of God. The second development of *kabbalah* is that of theosophy, which seeks to reveal the hidden life of God and the relationships between the Divine life, on the one hand, and the life of man and creation, on the other. Judaism has a long history of mysticism, dating back to rabbinic times. However, the early rabbis were not particularly supportive of mystic speculation, fearing that it could lead people away from Judaism.

It is believed that the *Zohar*, the *Book of Mystic Splendor*, was written in the late twelfth century. Its major aim was to explain God's commandments in a mystical way, dealing with the hidden meanings of the Bible. With the appearance of the *Zohar*, Jewish mysticism began to spread rapidly to European countries.

In 1492 the Jews of Spain were expelled, and the once great center of Jewish learning was in ruins. In the wake of this spiritual and physical upheaval, many Jews migrated to the Middle East. A number of them settled in the Upper Galilee, drawn to the town of Safed. It was here that a group of Jewish mystics was setting the stage for the numerous mystical movements of the next 400 years, among them the resurgence of interest in the study of *kabbalah*. Among the leaders of that community was Rabbi Isaac Luria, often referred to as Ha-Ari (the Lion) from the Hebrew initials of the words HaElohi Rabbi Yitchak (The Divine Rabbi Isaac). He developed a new system for understanding the mysteries of the *Zohar*. It became known as the Lurianic method and shed new light on the hidden wisdom of the *kabbalah*.

Isaac Luria was born of German parents in Jerusalem in 1534. While Luria was still a child his father died, and he was raised by his uncle Mordecai Francis, who placed him under the best Jewish teachers. He soon showed himself to be a diligent student of rabbinic literature.

In his early twenties Luria became engrossed with the study of the *Zohar*, the book of Jewish mysticism, which had recently been printed for the first time. Adopting the life of a hermit, he secluded himself for seven years, giving himself up entirely to meditation.

During that time he became a visionary, asserting that while asleep his soul ascended to heaven and conversed with great teachers of the past.

In 1569 Luria went to Israel, where after a short sojourn in Jerusalem he settled in Safed in the north. There he formed a circle of kabbalists to whom he imparted the doctrines by means of which he hoped to establish on a new basis the moral system of the world. To this circle belonged the likes of Moses Cordovero, Solomon Alkabiz, Joseph Karo (author of the Shulchan Aruch—The Code of Jewish Law), and Chayim Vital. His circle of students gradually widened, and soon his followers looked upon Luria as a miracle worker.

According to Luria scholars, he did not write anything, but rather the real exponent of his kabbalistic system was Chayim Vital, who collected the notes of the lectures from which were produced numerous works. Luria died in Safed in 1572. A synagogue in Safed named the Ha-Ari after him continues to be a popular tourist attraction.

LURIA'S KABBALISTIC GOD

Kabbalists maintain that God is unknowable to the human mind. They further believe that God is unlimited and infinite, often referring to God as the Ein Sof (The Infinite One).

The kabbalistic system teaches that God is manifested or revealed through intermediary agents. These are called Divine *sefirot*—luminaries or spheres from which God emanated. The order of the spheres is: *keter* (crown); *chochmah* (wisdom), the first real manifestation of God, containing the ideal plan of all the worlds; *binah* (understanding), that is, Divine intelligence in which the hidden pattern achieves concreteness; *chesed* (mercy) from which flow the merciful qualities of God; *gevurah* (power), the source of Divine judgment and law; *tiferet* (beauty), mediating between *chesed* and *gevurah* to bring harmony and compassion upon the world; *netzach* (eternity); *hod* (majesty); *yesod* (foundation), which concentrates all the higher power and influences; and *malchut* (kingdom), the receptive or "female" potency that distributes the Divine stream to the lower worlds.

Meditation, prayer, study, and contemplation are ways for

kabbalists to gain knowledge about God and how God relates to the world.

LURIA'S THREE STAGES OF CREATION

One of Luria's great contributions to Jewish thought was his doctrine of the three stages of creation. The following is a summary of that doctrine:

1. *Tzimtzum* (contraction): Since God was everywhere, Luria wondered how it was possible that there was space for anything to coexist with God. This question led Luria to the doctrine of *tzimtzum*, which means withdrawal or retreat. According to Luria, God contracted Himself and withdrew in order for the world to exist. By this act of withdrawal, God made room for the world by retreating from a portion of His universe. By retreating, God gave the people freedom to exist on their own and to choose between good and evil. Why did God create a world in which evil was even a possibility? Why did God not create a world that was perfectly good? The next two parts of Luria's theory were attempts to answer these questions.

2. *Shevirat HaKelim* (breaking of the vessels): Luria used myths and symbols to explain his theory. The story that Luria told was a myth that attempted to explain why God had allowed the terrible suffering and tragedy of exile from Spain that occurred in 1492. Luria's myth was called "the breaking of the vessels." According to his myth, there is a flaw in the world. The reason for the flaw lies in what happened after God withdrew to allow the creation of the world. God created and destroyed many worlds. The first worlds that God created were destroyed because the light that came forth from God was too strong and powerful for people. The first worlds that God created after His retreat were called vessels. The

destruction of these worlds was called "the breaking of the vessels." This cosmic catastrophe preceded the creation of our world.

Because of this accident, the world we live in is imperfect. Broken fragments of these vessels have fallen into our world. These broken vessels, called *kelippot* (shells) are symbolic of evil. Evil breaks the order of the world, and everything in the world becomes a series of broken fragments. The exile of the Jews from Spain was like the broken fragments, having moved the Jewish people from their place. The whole world, as Luria viewed it, was flawed. It was not the way it ought to be.

3. *Tikkun* (repair of the world): Luria believed that God intended the world to be good. But since man had the right to choose, evil was a possibility, and that is why God allowed the breaking of the vessels to occur. But God also gave man the power to combat evil. Sparks of light are symbolic of God's presence, and Luria believed that sparks of God's presence existed in the world. However, these Divine sparks were imprisoned in the *kelippot*, the broken fragments of the vessels. It is the task of the Jew, according to Luria, to free these scattered sparks from their shells and to reunite them with God.

This myth thus gave purpose to the suffering of the exiled Spanish Jews. The purpose of the exile was to extract the last sparks of godliness and to find the good within the world. By searching for God, man can restore and repair the world to its original state of peace and harmony. The process of mending the world is called *tikkun*. Mending of the world can be accomplished through the performance of the mitzvot— God's commandments. The repair of the world can also be accomplished through prayer. True prayer, rendered with proper concentration and intention, says Luria, will allow a person's soul to ascend and commune with God. The sign that complete *tikkun* has occurred will be the coming of the Messiah.

LURIA'S FIVE SOULS

According to Luria, the *sefirot* were transformed into "figures." The first *sefirah*, *keter* (crown), was transformed into the potentially existing three heads of the Macroprosopon; the second *sefirah*, *chochmah* (wisdom), was transformed into the active masculine principle called "Father"; the third *sefirah*, *binah* (wisdom), became the passive, feminine principle called "Mother"; the six broken *sefirot* were transformed into the male child, which is the product of the masculine active and the feminine passive principles; the tenth *sefirah*, *malchut* (kingdom), was transformed into the female child. This procedure was absolutely necessary, for if God in the beginning had created these figures instead of the *sefirot*, there would have been no evil in the world, and consequently no reward and punishment. For the source of evil is the broken *sefirot* or vessels, while the light of the Ein Sof produces only that which is good.

These five figures are found in each of the worlds: world of emanation, world of creation, world of formation, and world of action, which represents the material world.

From the five figures, Luria says emanated five souls. From highest to lowest they are: *neshamah, ruach, nefesh, chaya,* and *yechidah*. Man's soul is the connecting link between the infinite and the finite. According to Luria, all the souls destined for the human race were created together with the various organs of Adam. Each human soul is a spark from Adam. The first sin of Adam caused confusion among the various classes of souls. The superior intermingled with the inferior, so that even the purest soul received a mixture of evil or, as Luria calls it, of the element of "shells" (*kelippot*). From the lowest classes of souls proceeded the pagan world, while from the higher emanated the Israelite world. The state of confusion among souls will one day cease when the Messiah arrives, for the Messiah will establish the new moral system upon which the world will be based. Until that time man's soul must wander through the bodies of animals, humans, and inanimate things such as stone and wood.

According to Luria, every person bears on his or her forehead a mark by which one may learn the nature of his or her soul, to which degree and class it belongs, the wanderings it has already accomplished, and to which soul it should be united in order to become fully purified. This union can be effected by formulas of conjuration.

IN SUMMATION

Mysticism, although discouraged by early rabbinic thinkers, has continued to shine its influence upon Jewish thinkers. For mystics, God exists and is unknowable, unlimited, and infinite. The ten *sefirot* (Divine emanations) provide the necessary bridge to the gap between the unknowable God and the known universe. Isaac Luria preferred a world where man was free to choose, even if this meant the possibility of evil. Luria's theory of God's contraction allows room for physical things in the world.

Luria also introduced his mystic system into religious observances. Every commandment had for him a mystical meaning. The Sabbath with all its ceremonies was looked upon as the embodiment of the Divinity in temporal life. Every ceremony performed on the holy Sabbath was considered to have an influence upon the superior world.

Finally, the mission of the Jewish people is to help mend the world (through performance of God's commandments) by gathering the Divine sparks that have been scattered throughout the universe. The complete repair of the world will hasten the coming of the Messiah.

16

PANTHEISM AND BARUCH SPINOZA

BACKGROUND

Modern Jewish philosophy shared with Hellenistic and medieval Jewish philosophy a concern for relating general philosophy to Judaism. It did, however, differ from Hellenistic and medieval Jewish philosophy in several ways. For one thing, it differed in its conception of Jewish tradition. For Hellenistic and medieval Jewish philosophy, Judaism, with its oral and written law, was the revealed word of God, which was forever binding on the people. While some modern Jewish thinkers accepted this traditionalist opinion, most considered Judaism a creation of human thought.

One of the greatest philosophers of the entire western philosophic tradition was Baruch Spinoza. Born in 1632 in Amsterdam, this Dutch philosopher was an exemplary student of the Spanish-Portuguese community. Several claims have been made regarding how Spinoza was led to his irreligious views. One claim suggests that Spinoza studied with the ex-Jesuit Van den Enden, while another suggests that his irreverence stemmed from the heretical controversies within the Amsterdam Jewish community. In 1656 Spinoza began to attract considerable attention for his unorthodox opinions, in which he questioned Moses' authorship of the Torah, whether Adam was the first man, and whether Mosaic law superseded natural law. For these views and others, Spinoza was excommunicated, and the Jewish community was forbidden to be in contact with him.

In 1660 Spinoza left Amsterdam, changed his name to Benedictus (Latin for Baruch), and became involved with liberal Protestants. The noted historian Arthur Hertzberg has described Spinoza as the first modern Jew because he was the first to leave the Jewish community without becoming a Christian.

In 1670 he wrote his *Tractatus Theologico-Politicus* in which he critiqued revealed religion, presented his justification for intellectual freedom, and outlined his political theories. This work was said to initiate modern Bible criticism, pointing to internal contradictions. In it he draws the difference between theology, the obedient knowledge of faith and piety, and philosophy, the independent rational discovery of truth in nature. He opposed clerical authority and the claims made in behalf of revelation and argued that the state must ensure free thought. Because of this work, Spinoza was accused of being an atheist.

In 1673 Spinoza was offered the chair of philosophy at Heidelberg but declined, preferring private research rather than public teaching.

By 1674 Spinoza had completed his major work, the *Ethics*. He was unable to get his work published, because it denied the existence of God. After continuing to write and research philosophy, he died of consumption in 1677.

SPINOZA'S PHILOSOPHY

Spinoza has been regarded as the one modern philosopher whose life is harmoniously bound with his theory. Spinoza's simple and moral life, devoted to rational enquiry, developed out of his rejection of ceremonial Judaism and his efforts to find a basis for rejecting scriptural authority. He insisted that religious tenets should be judged only on the basis of reason, and he rejected Moses as the author of the Torah and the possibility of genuine prophecy. He offered a rationalistic metaphysics within which supernatural events could not occur, and within which the Bible was to be examined as a human document expressing human developments of the past.

Asserting that miracles were impossible, Spinoza posited that nature is governed by eternal decrees of God, and nothing could be contrary to God's natural laws. Since God determined nature within the parameters of His law, nothing supernatural was possible. Biblical moral teachings, in Spinoza's view, were simply compatible with those of reason.

GOD'S NATURE

The first book of the *Ethics* develops Spinoza's theory of substance ("that which is in itself, and is conceived through itself"), insisting first on its unity and simplicity. Spinoza concluded that God or Nature is the only possible substance, and that everything in the world is an aspect of God. His pantheistic theology thus maintained that God and the universe are one. God is nature, the laws of nature were set by God, and everything follows their structure. God does not act independently of the world, for God is the world.

For Spinoza, God is not a purposeful being. There are no goals being achieved. God just is, and due to His being, everything happens of necessity. Man's ultimate aim is the intellectual love of God, which can give man the continuous and unending happiness that was sought. Thus the philosophic goal of complete wisdom becomes man's salvation.

BODY AND MIND

Book 2 of Spinoza's *Ethics* continues to expand upon his theology. For Spinoza, everything is in God, who is modified in terms of His two known attributes: thought and extension. The worlds of body and of mind are two aspects of God or Nature. The order and connection of ideas are the same as the order and connection of things. The latter can be understood in terms of mathematical physics, the former in terms of logic and psychology, but both are ways of understanding the same substance, namely God. Thus the mind and the body are essentially the same thing.

KNOWLEDGE

For Spinoza, man, through the course of experience, develops general ideas of what is going on in the world, and through these, a level of scientific understanding of the sequence of events taking place. From these man comes to adequate ideas, which gives him a logical understanding. The highest form of knowledge, according to Spinoza, would be to have a complete understanding, to see everything as a logical system from the aspect of eternity. This intuitive knowledge is only completely possessed by God. Complete understanding would be to know the infinite idea of God, which man can only approach but never fully know.

MAN'S FREEDOM

Spinoza asserts that man is driven toward self-preservation, constantly affected by the emotions in the form of pleasure and pain. On this level man is in human bondage, moved by causes that he does not understand.

As man begins to understand what is going on in his life, he achieves human freedom. Freedom for Spinoza consists not in being uncaused, but in being determined by oneself alone. When a person understands why things are happening and knows that they cannot be otherwise, that person is liberated from bondage to ignorance.

The understanding that gives a person freedom is the highest good. As one reaches the stage of rational understanding, one's ideas become part of the infinite idea of God. Man's ultimate aim, says Spinoza, is the intellectual love of God, which can bring unending happiness. Thus the philosophic goal of complete wisdom becomes man's salvation.

POLITICAL THEORY

Spinoza's political theory holds that the aim of the good society is that of allowing rational men to think freely and achieve true knowledge. To achieve this requires civil peace, allowing for free thought.

According to Spinoza, for unenlightened people (such as the Jewish people), the conveying of moral teachings by stories, alleged prophecy, and promises can have an important social effect of making people behave better and obey laws. But Spinoza asserts, the wise man needs only the religion of reason.

Spinoza's completely rationalistic vision incorporates some basic themes: the existence and unity of God, the dependence of all things on God, and the love of God as the basis of morality. His view, however, is the first modern one to provide a metaphysical basis for rejecting any form of Judaism or Christianity portraying the human scene as a dramatic interplay of man and God. The denial of the possibility of any supreme event or revelatory knowledge eliminated the basic written and oral traditions so that they no longer provided any essential data about man's relationship to God.

SPINOZA AS BIBLE COMMENTATOR

Spinoza's biblical criticism is closely connected with his philosophic system and political position. He developed what he saw to be the true method of biblical interpretation, namely that the Bible must be interpreted on its own terms. Spinoza asserts that the history of the Bible should consist of three aspects: an analysis of Hebrew language, the compilation and classification of the expressions of each of the biblical books, and research as to the origins of the biblical writings. Spinoza also analyzed the biblical books in an attempt to determine their authors.

According to Spinoza, some of the first five books of the Bible did originate with Moses, although it was centuries after Moses that the Pentateuch as a whole appeared. The Pentateuch, together with the Books of Joshua, Judges, Samuel, and Kings, forms a single larger historical work whose author, Spinoza posits, was Ezra.

According to Spinoza, biblical stories are never to be believed literally, but rather are intended to instruct the people, since they had difficulty understanding abstract concepts. Finally, since nothing can happen that contradicts natural law, biblical miracle stories must always be explained in a natural way.

IN SUMMATION

Spinoza's philosophic tenets provide the foundations for a kind of atheism in which the historical interrelationship of God and man is denied. Of all the sixteenth- and seventeenth-century critics of both Judaism and Christianity, Spinoza alone seems to have taken the drastic step of replacing religious tradition completely by rational, scientific reasoning. During the 1950s Israeli Prime Minister David ben Gurion suggested that the writ excommunication of Spinoza be withdrawn retroactively. The Amsterdam rabbis did not act on ben Gurion's motion.

Spinoza has been described as "the most impious atheist that ever lived on the face of the earth" and also as a "God-intoxicated man." His theory provides the foundation for a kind of atheism in which the interrelationship of God and man is denied, and in which God has no personality whatsoever. His revolutionary steps replaced religious tradition by rational, scientific study. His main influence was on biblical critics, deists, and eighteenth-century French atheists, and his ideas have been seen as precursors of Marxism.

17

MOSES MENDELSSOHN

BACKGROUND

Moses Mendelssohn, philosopher, commentator, and translator of the Bible, was known as "the third Moses." Born in 1729 in Dessau, he was also called Moses Dessau, after his birthplace. His Hebrew name was Moses ben Menachem-Mendel, abbreviated by the acronym RaMBeMaN. The son of a Torah scribe, he received a strong traditional Jewish education under the influence of the Rabbi of Dessau, David Fraenkel. In 1743 he went to Berlin, where Rabbi Fraenkel had been called as rabbi several months earlier. His teachers included Israel Zamosz who taught him math, and Abraham Kisch who was his teacher in Latin.

Most of Mendelssohn's writings deal with matters of general philosophy, rather than with particularly Jewish issues. In 1754 Mendelssohn began to publish philosophic writings and literary reviews with the assistance of G. E. Lessing, a writer and dramatist who became his lifetime friend. In 1763 he was awarded the first prize of the Prussian Royal Academy of Sciences for his work

Abhandlung ueber die Evidenz in metaphysischen Wissenschaften. Interestingly, one of the other philosophers who competed in the competition was the philosopher Immanuel Kant. In 1770 he published an annotated edition of the Book of Ecclesiastes and composed a commentary on Maimonides' *Logic* entitled *Millot Hahiggayon*. By 1783 he had completed his German translation of the *Five Books of Moses* with commentary, called the *Biur*. This work proved of great significance in the process of Jewish Enlightenment.

In 1783 Mendelssohn composed his *Jerusalem*, renowned for its analysis of Judaism and its vigorous defense of tolerance. He died in Berlin in 1786.

PHILOSOPHY OF RELIGION

As a philosopher of religion, Mendelssohn did not create an original system. Instead, he continued in the tradition of classical rationalism that was current in the seventeenth and eighteenth centuries. His philosophy incorporates the major themes of Enlightenment philosophy: its emphasis on reason as the sole medium by which man acquires knowledge fulfillment; the notion that man is endowed with eternally valid innate ideas of absolute goodness and truth; and the purpose of philosophy not as the discovery of truth but as the achievement of happiness by the individual and society through the perfection of man.

Mendelssohn's philosophic starting point is his theory of knowledge. He distinguishes between eternal truths, which are self-evident to reason, and historical, temporal truths, requiring the evidence of sense experience. Among the truths self-evident to reason are the belief in a wise and merciful God and the immortality of the human soul. These metaphysical truths are the themes of his two major works, *Morgenstunden* (1785) and *Phaedon* (1767). In the former he seeks to demonstrate the rationality of the belief in the existence of God and treats the subject as a principle of man's universal religion of reason. In his work *Phaedon*, Mendelssohn deals with the immortality of the soul.

GOD'S EXISTENCE

Mendelssohn's most used proof for God's existence is a modification of the ontological argument: Man finds the idea of a Supreme Being in his consciousness. Since this idea cannot have arisen out of man's limited experiences, we have no direct knowledge of anything remotely resembling the idea of divine perfection—it is *a priori* and belongs to the category of concepts that precede all experience and enable us to comprehend the universe. Although these concepts do not arise from experience, they are not subjective because they determine the character of universal experience. Further, there is a necessary connection between the concept of a perfect being and his existence. A being that is absolutely perfect must have existence among its attributes. Otherwise, it would be lacking the full complement of its unconditioned possibility.

IMMORTALITY OF THE SOUL

The question of the immortality of the soul is fully examined in Mendelssohn's chief philosophic work *Phaedon*, modeled on Plato's dialogue of the same name. Mendelssohn posited that an infinite number of souls constitute the inner substance of the universe. Things that perish do not cease to exist. Rather, they are dissolved into their elements. The soul is one such element, since it is the soul that imposes a unifying pattern on the changing elements of the body. Thus the soul can neither weaken by age nor perish through death.

It is through the goodness of God that each soul will retain its consciousness in a future state. It is God who has implanted in man the idea that the soul is immortal. To assume otherwise would be incongruous with God's goodness and justice.

MAN'S FREEDOM OF CHOICE

Mendelssohn's belief in God's existence and the immortality of the soul is in harmony with the prevalent views of Jewish tradition. He does differ, however, in his conception of free will. Inasmuch as every act of will must have a cause or reason, human freedom, if defined as an uncaused act, is logically impossible. Man's will can only be free in the sense that it is determined by a recognition of the good. But if man is not truly free, the sinner cannot be responsible for his or her misdeeds. If this be the case, then why, Mendelssohn queries, should man be punished? Mendelssohn answers that divine punishment is not an end in itself. Rather, it is a means of cleansing transgressors in order to prepare them for life in the world to come. Divine justice is superseded by divine goodness, which never excludes man permanently from the bliss of eternal life.

CIVIL RIGHTS

Mendelssohn was very conscious of living in Exile and being a person without a homeland. From the 1770s he became actively involved in the struggle for the protection and the civil rights of the Jews. He also assisted Jewish communities involved in conflicts with the authorities, taking advantage of his recognized status in order to request help from people whom he befriended. Interestingly, Mendelssohn was not always in agreement with the rabbis. In 1772 he advised the Jews of Mecklenburg to consent to the demand of authorities to arrange the burial of the dead after three days because this practice did not violate Torah law and was even to be recommended on religious grounds. His opinion was rejected by the rabbis. Mendelssohn also rejected autonomous Jewish jurisdiction, calling for government-appointed judges to whom one would turn, without any relation to his religious attachment.

MENDELSSOHN ON JUDAISM

Following the approach of the Enlightenment, Mendelssohn maintains that if the true doctrines of religion are based on reason, divine revelation is no longer needed as a source of truth. Here Mendelssohn deviates sharply from Maimonides, for whom man's knowledge of truth is derived from both reason and revelation.

Mendelssohn asserts that if Judaism is revealed, it cannot be a religion, and if Judaism is a religion, it cannot have been revealed. Mendelssohn solves this dilemma by defining Judaism not as a "revealed religion" but as "revealed law." The central religious tenets of Judaism (the existence and unity of God and the immortality of the soul) are not specific Jewish notions but doctrines of the general religion of reason, which require no act of revelation to be understood. For Mendelssohn, what distinguishes the Jew from the non-Jew is not one's religion, which is the common property of all people of reason, but the unique laws and commandments that were disclosed at Mount Sinai. That God spoke at Sinai is a historical fact for Mendelssohn, because it was witnessed by an entire Israelite people. All people are destined to attain gratification, but Jews can attain it only by observing the Sinaitic laws.

ATTITUDE TOWARD CHRISTIANITY

Mendelssohn concluded that Judaism does not possess dogmas. Rather, it addresses itself to man's will but does not attempt to control his thoughts. On the other hand, Christianity, he asserted, is based on dogmas that are opposed to reason. Mendelssohn vehemently objects to its claim that only those who believe in Jesus and his miracles can perceive the truth and are worthy of eternal bliss. Also, the Christian interpretations of the words of the Jewish prophets, which purportedly herald the coming of Jesus are, in his opinion, totally unfounded.

IN SUMMATION

Mendelssohn's death was greatly mourned by Jews and non-Jews alike. Becoming a legend in his own lifetime, he was regarded as the embodiment of the humanist ideal. As a great defender of Judaism, he sought to prove that it could withstand the test of rationalist inquiry. However, the strength of the rationalism upon which he based himself was unable to span the gulf between traditional Judaism and the world of rationalistic thought. His life thus became a testimony of the basic conflict of the emancipation—the conflict between assimilation and the safeguarding of the singularity of Jewish life.

The movement developed by Mendelssohn's disciples became known as Haskalah (Enlightenment). They tried to bring about a Jewish cultural renaissance, which would draw on the best to be found both within Judaism and in the secular world. Decades later, the Haskalah movement spread from Western Europe to the Jews of Russia and Poland.

The celebration in 1829 of the hundredth anniversary of his birth included the erecting of a monument in the city of Dessau to his memory. In his memory one of Mendelssohn's great-grandsons established a scholarship fund at the University of Berlin.

18

Samuel David Luzzatto

BACKGROUND

Often referred to by the acronym of SHaDaL, this Italian scholar and philosopher was born in 1800, claiming descent from a long line of Luzzatto scholars. In 1821 his translation of the Ashkenazi prayer book into Italian appeared, and in 1829 he was appointed professor of the rabbinic college of Padua. There he spent the rest of his life teaching Bible, philosophy, and Jewish history. The scope of his learning is demonstrated in the mass of letters written to outstanding Jewish scholars of the day. Over 700 of these letters were published, and some are in themselves dissertations. Luzzatto wrote a Hebrew commentary on the *Five Books of Moses* with Italian translation in the early 1870s. He also did pioneering work in his editions of Judah Halevi's poetry and medieval poetry. In 1841 he published a work entitled *Avnai Zikkaron* (*Stones of Remembrance*), being among the first to treat epitaphs as an important primary source for Jewish historical research.

ATTITUDES TOWARD JUDAISM

Luzzatto wrote a lengthy dissertation in Hebrew on the Book of Ecclesiastes. It is in this type of work that his attitude toward Judaism is revealed. He was basically a traditionalist who had a great reverence for the medieval commentator Rashi. His antagonism toward Abraham ibn Ezra is readily apparent in his letters and Bible commentaries. Luzzatto divided seekers of truth into two groups: those who follow Rashi and Samuel ben Meir and those who are the disciples of Maimonides and ibn Ezra (Letter numbers 272 and 275). His own commentary on the *Five Books of Moses* is not fundamentalist; whereas he himself did not take the first chapters of the Book of Genesis literally, he criticizes those who treat them as an allegory. He believed them to be meant as model lessons from which we are to derive moral and ethical values.

Luzzatto was one of the first Jewish scholars to turn his attention to Syriac, considering a knowledge of this language necessary for the understanding of the Targum. He was also, according to some historians, the first Jew who permitted himself to amend the text of the Tanach, and his emendations often met with the approval of Christian scholars. Through a careful examination of the Book of Ecclesiastes, Luzzatto concluded that its author was not Solomon, but someone who lived several centuries later and whose name was Kohelet. As to the Book of Isaiah, in spite of the prevalent opinion that chapters forty through fifty-six were written after the Babylonian captivity, Luzzatto maintained that the whole book was written by Isaiah.

Luzzatto maintained a firm belief in revelation and treated the Torah text with sacred regard. He had the highest regard for the Aramaic translation of Onkelos to which he devoted his work *Ohev Ger (Lover of the Proselyte)*.

PHILOSOPHY

Luzzatto was a warm defender of biblical and Talmudic Judaism. His opposition to philosophic Judaism brought him many adversaries among his contemporaries. But his opposition to philosophy was not the result of fanaticism nor of lack of understanding. He claimed to have read all the ancient philosophers and that the more he read them the more he found them deviating from the truth.

Luzzatto's philosophy may be compared with that of Judah Halevi. He had high regard for the great philosopher Maimonides but listed his objections to Maimonides' *Guide of the Perplexed* and to some remarks in *Sefer HaMadda*. He attacked Abraham ibn Ezra, declaring that his works were not the products of a scientific mind. He was opposed to Maimonides' enumeration and formulation of the Thirteen Principles of Faith and his condemnation to those who did not subscribe to them. His attitude toward Greek philosophy was negative and quite antagonistic. He reacted negatively to kabbalistic mysticism and blamed rationalistic philosophy for having brought about, as a reaction, the flowering of the mystical movement.

In his theological writings, most of them published as lectures, he developed his own positive system of Jewish theology and religious philosophy, based on the firm belief in revelation, tradition, and the election of Israel. He maintained that the Torah and its *mitzvot* must not be rationalized, nor can morality be separated from religion. They both flow from the same innate human quality of empathy. He also posited that the Jewish people are both the carrier and guarantor of this revealed, national religion that embodies its own universalism and humanitarianism. Hebrew language and literature, the main object of Luzzatto's scholarly work, help to foster and deepen Jewish spirit and loyalties. This nationalistic conception of Judaism embraces a sort of religious Zionism.

IN SUMMATION

During his literary career of more than fifty years, Luzzatto wrote a great number of works, both in Hebrew and in Italian. He was a constant contributor to most of the Hebrew and Jewish periodicals of his time.

His biblical commentaries continued to be used and studied by students throughout the world. He also was probably one of the most erudite Hebrew philologists of the nineteenth century.

19

NEO-ORTHODOXY AND SAMSON RAPHAEL HIRSCH

BACKGROUND

Born in 1808, Hirsch was a rabbi, leader, and foremost exponent of Orthodoxy in Germany in the nineteenth century. Born in Hamburg, he studied Talmud with his grandfather Mendel Frankfurter. There his education was influenced by the enlightened Orthodox rabbis Jacob Ettlinger and Isaac Bernays. In 1829 he attended the University of Bonn where he studied classical languages and philosophy. He there formed a friendship with Abraham Geiger and organized with him a society of students for study. The friendship of these two young scholars, the future leaders of two opposing movements (Orthodox and Reform) in German Jewry, was disrupted after Geiger published a sharp criticism of Hirsch's *Nineteen Letters* which professed his views of Judaism.

In 1841 Hirsch served as rabbi of Aurich and Osnabrueck in Hanover. In 1848 he was elected chairman of the Committee for the Civil and Political Rights of the Jews in Moravia. In 1851 he was called to serve as rabbi of the Orthodox congregation Adas Jeschurun in Frankfurt on the Main, a position he held for thirty-seven years until his death. It was here that he further developed his concept of Judaism, and the congregation embodied his new-Orthodox ideas. His synagogue continued to function after his death in 1888, until the Nazis destroyed the community a half-century later.

ATTITUDE TOWARD REFORM

The demand for reform was Judaism's chief contemporary problem. Reform advocates felt that Jews were prevented from being able to find a place within German society, due to distinctive dress, the Hebrew language of prayer, and other obligations that were becoming difficult to perform in a Christian society. In 1854 Hirsch published a pamphlet called "Die Religion im Bunde mit dem Fortschritt" ("Religion Allied with Progress") in which he refuted the argument of the Reform leaders that the combination of traditional Judaism and secular education was impossible. Hirsch maintained that there was a need to revise externals within Judaism. He introduced, for example, some external improvements in the liturgy, such as a choir under the direction of a professional music conductor, congregational singing, and sermonizing twice a month using German. However, he rejected any changes affecting principles of faith or alterations in Jewish law, which Reform leaders advocated. In Hirsch's opinion the Jews, rather than Judaism, were in need of reform. He further maintained that for Judaism to have access to the cultural life of Europe it was essential for Jews to rise to the eternal ideas of Judaism. He defended the Hebrew language as the sole language for prayer and instruction of Jewish subjects and opposed the Reform movement's rejection of the belief in the coming of the Return to Zion.

Unlike the Reform leader Geiger, who maintained that a true

separation between the Reform and Orthodox movements was a necessity, Hirsch maintained that such a schism ought to be avoided. However, when the rabbinic synod at Brunsick decided to annul several prohibitions, including those relating to dietary laws, Hirsch changed his attitude.

In 1885 Hirsch established the Freie Vereinigung fur die Interessen des orthodoxen Judentums ("The Free Society for the Advancement of the Interest of Orthodox Judaism") with its seat in Frankfurt.

JEWISH EDUCATION

Hirsch referred his educational ideal to the famous saying of Rabban Gamliel in the Ethics of the Fathers (2:2): "The study of the Torah is excellent when combined with *derech eretz*" (modern culture). For Hirsch, the ideal Jew was the Jissroelmensch ("Israel man"), a term that Hirsch himself coined, meaning an enlightened Jew who performed the commandments. The principle of Torah combined with *derech eretz* became the general slogan of Hirsch's congregation and others in Germany as well.

Hirsch founded three schools: a primary school, a secondary school, and a high school for girls. Besides the Hebrew language and Jewish subjects, the school curriculum included secular studies (e.g., German, mathematics, and natural sciences). It was clear that Hirsch felt that a Jewish education consisted of both religious and secular education.

HIRSCH'S CONCEPTION OF JUDAISM

Hirsch's views on the essential content of Judaism led him to oppose the conception of the historical development of Judaism as conceived by Graetz and Zechariah Frankel. Hirsch regarded genuine Judaism as the expression of Divinity revealed in nature and in the Torah. According to Hirsch, since the Torah, like nature, is a fact, no principle revealed in it may be denied even when it is beyond man's powers of understanding. It is incumbent upon man to search for the revelation of God's wisdom in the Torah, as in nature. The existence of this wisdom is contained in the commandments, and the character of the Torah as an objective reality lies in the fact that its central axis is the Law. The Law is never dependent on the will of the individual or society, nor on historical processes. According to Hirsch, a single people, namely the Jewish people, was created to whom the religious truth was given directly. Since this people recognized this truth from the outset, it has no need for experiences acquired in time in order to learn it.

HIRSCH'S VIEW OF THE COMMANDMENTS

Hirsch developed a system for explaining the commandments based on two methods: (1) the method of speculative etymology or philosophic etymology, which attempts to discover the intellectual conception of a word, and (2) the symbolic method that seeks to demonstrate that the commandment is not determined by simple devotion but by attachment to the religious thought represented in symbolic form by the commandment. Symbolic meanings must be attributed to the following: (1) commandments that are described in the Torah itself as signs (*otot*), such as circumcision, putting on *tefillin*, and Sabbath rest; (2) commandments established as pointing to historical events, such as *matzah* and the *sukkah*; and (3) commandments whose entire content testifies to their symbolic character, such as the red heifer (Deuteronomy 21:1–19).

Hirsch's two-volume *Horeb* explained the 613 commandments. He arranged the commandments under six headings: teachings (the principles of Jewish faith), decisions (concerning the relations of man to man), ordinances (revelations of man

to animal, vegetable, and inanimate kingdoms), commandments (concerning the love of all created things), testimonies
(mnemonic signs), and worship (prayer and sacrifice). Hirsch
maintained that all the commandments can be reduced to three
basic principles: justice, love, and the education of ourselves and
others.

BIBLE TRANSLATION

Hirsch translated the *Five Books of Moses* and also wrote a
commentary on them. His translation of the Bible into German
was a literal one, and in its faithfulness to the details of the
original it goes so far as to employ forms that are foreign to
the spirit of the German language. Buber's translation of the
Bible into German bears a resemblance in methodology to that
of Hirsch. Hirsch rejected the aesthetic approach in his translation, stating that the Bible addresses itself to the intellect and
leaves little room for the workings of the imagination. He also
rejected the methods of biblical interpretation based on the
context in time and space.

THE JEWISH PEOPLE

Whereas the Reform leaders attempted to demonstrate that
Judaism was only a religious sect, Hirsch maintained that God
had established Israel as a people and not as a religious congregation. In his writings Hirsch employs the concept "national
Jewish consciousness." In his opinion, the Jewish people will
never find true spiritual development other than in the Holy
Land. He maintains that Israel's mission is to teach the nations
that God is the source of blessing. For this reason Israel was
given both the Land and God's blessings. These views continued
to be expounded by others, and in the course of time became

the ideological basis for the Agudat Israel (World Organization of Orthodox Jews).

IN SUMMATION

Hirsch's importance as a religious spiritual leader and his wide influence as a teacher, organizer, and writer made him a champion of Orthodoxy in its controversy with liberal Judaism. While advocating strict adherence to Jewish law, he tried to find a solution to the political and cultural challenges presented in modern life to Judaism.

When thousands of German Jews escaped to the United States during the 1930s, many of Hirsch's followers settled in Manhattan, New York's Washington Heights. Even today, more than a century after his death, the area continues to remain a place that espouses his Orthodox teachings. Today Hirsch is generally regarded as the progenitor of neo-Orthodoxy in western countries, aspiring to fuse European culture with unqualified loyalty to rigorously observed traditional Judaism.

20

REFORM JUDAISM AND ABRAHAM GEIGER

BACKGROUND

Born in 1810, Geiger was a rabbi and one of the early leaders of the Reform movement in Judaism. He was an outstanding scholar of Wissenschaft des Judentums (literally the "science of Judaism," referring to the scientific, critical study of Judaism using modern methods of research). Geiger received a traditional Jewish education. In Bonn, Germany he became acquainted with his future Orthodox adversary Samson Raphael Hirsch with whom he set up a young men's circle of study for purposes of preaching. In 1832 he became rabbi in Wiesbaden, where he took his first steps to introduce reform of the synagogue services. In 1837 he convened the first meeting of Reform rabbis in Wiesbaden.

In 1838 Geiger was chosen as *dayyan* and assistant rabbi by the Breslau community. There he established a school for religious studies and a group for study of Hebrew philology.

Geiger was one of the active participants in the synods held by the Reform rabbis in Frankfurt and Breslau. From 1863 he served as rabbi of the Reform congregation in his hometown of Frankfurt. In 1872 the Hochschule für die Wissenschaft (center for the scientific study of Judaism) was established with Geiger's assistance, and Geiger directed it until his death in 1874.

PHILOSOPHY

During his lifetime Geiger combined the work of a reforming theologian and a philologist-historian. His scientific research ranged over almost every sphere of Judaism. His personal knowledge of both Jewish and general subjects served his aspiration to make Judaism an integral part of the general European culture in its German context.

Geiger valued prophecy in Judaism, but he was radically opposed to Orthodoxy, maintaining that it was lacking in aesthetic forms to satisfy the cultured man. He aspired to lead Jewry to a type of assimilation that would further fulfillment of the Jewish mission to spread rational faith in the One God and God's moral law, and also would lead to a modification of the Jewish way of life.

Geiger set out to eliminate from Judaism every mark of national uniqueness. His attitude was negative toward all manifestations of Jewish solidarity. He opposed prayer services in Hebrew, which he justified by pointing out the ignorance of the language among most worshipers. He omitted all references to Return to Zion from the prayer book that he brought out for the Breslau community, while retaining Hebrew corresponding in its essentials with the original version alongside several prayers in German. He also changed the German translation accompanying the prayers, in accordance with Reform theology (for example, reviver of the dead is translated in his version as "source of eternal life," since reform theology generally denies a physical afterlife). He did not agree to changing the Sabbath to

Sunday, even though he did permit instrumental music on the Sabbath in the synagogue.

Geiger considerably shortened the order of prayer in an attempt to enable worshipers to pray with more fervor and devotion. Interestingly, he established prayers for rain in summer also, to suit conditions in Germany.

GEIGER'S WRITINGS

In his doctoral thesis *Was hat Mohammed aus dem Judenthume aufgenommen*, Geiger demonstrated the influence of Jewish tradition upon the Koran. In his principal work, *Urschrift und Uebersetzungen der Bibel*, he correlates the history of the biblical translations with the history of the various sects in Israel, particularly the Pharisees and Sadducees.

Other writings included a study of Maimonides, translations of poems by Judah Halevi and ibn Gabirol, and a study on Leone Modena.

IN SUMMATION

Geiger succeeded in making Judaism an integral part of the general European culture in its German context. His scholarly works on the Bible and its translations continue to be studied by scholars throughout the world. It is clear that he helped pave the way for the modern Reform branch of Judaism that we know today. Geiger's great hope was that Reform Judaism would be served by many rabbis of equal scholarship. Having worked for the establishment of a seminary for rabbis in Breslau, he was obviously disappointed when he was not asked to become its director.

One statement in particular sums up Geiger's philosophy of life: "To draw from the past, live for the present, and to work for the future."

21

ISRAEL SALANTER

BACKGROUND

Israel Salanter, born in 1801 in Zhagory, is the founder and the spiritual father of the Musar movement. The biblical word *musar* is often used in the sense of moral instruction. During the medieval period, the term *musar* gradually acquired the connotation of moral principles that tend to improve the relation of man to man. Salanter's primary concern in his own life and teachings was ethics. Fearing that the moral fiber of Jewish communities was being weakened by external forces, he advocated that the curriculum in the Jewish schools emphasize the study of ethical literature. A life devoted to contemplation, religious fervor, and self-sacrifice, leading to exemplary ethical conduct, was the primary goal of the "Musarnicks," as they were called.

Early in his life he accepted the position of head of a *yeshivah* in Vilna. Later he established his own *yeshivah* there, and when his fame spread he began to preach sermons giving expression to the doctrine of *musar*, a moral movement based on the study of traditional ethical literature. These sermons attracted extremely large audiences, and soon Salanter set up special Musar houses for the study of Jewish ethical literature.

In 1857 Salanter moved to Germany where he lectured to university students on Judaism. During this period he continued to maintain contact with his students in Lithuania by correspondence. These letters constitute the main source for his system of *musar*.

In 1880 he went to France in order to disseminate Judaism. He stayed in Paris for two years and succeeded in strengthening its Jewish institutions. From Paris he returned to Koenigsberg where he died in 1883.

ETHICAL IDEAS

Israel Salanter believed (to some extent he anticipated Freud) that people have forces in their souls that lie beneath the level of the conscious, rational mind and that these forces really influence peoples' lives. It is not useful, he maintained, merely to read the Musar ethical literature, because that will not have a lasting effect on conduct. In order to get down, as it were, into the subconscious mind, a constant repetition of Musar ethical themes is needed. If, for example, a person is becoming proud and vain, to eradicate these traits he must repeat over and over again verses about the folly of pride. Salanter believed that by repeated chantings, an abhorrence of these undesirable traits becomes habitual and one becomes more humble. Salanter always demanded of his followers a ruthless self-criticism leading to sound ethical conduct.

The following is a cross section of the ethical teachings of Israel Salanter, based on his writings:

1. The sensual desire in a person often makes him mistake momentary pleasure for the true happiness that he craves, and he succumbs to the pressure of his passion. Frequent yielding to his sensual desires finally produces in man an impure spirit—the decay of his spiritual energy—with the result that he becomes a slave to his evil habits.

2. The moral clearsightedness commands man to struggle against the temptation of sensual desires and to be guided in his actions not by the immediate pleasures that they produce but by their remote consequences. Without deep sincerity we would find little to criticize in ourselves; self-love would blind our judgment. Repentance is not remorse but a serious attempt to profit from past mistakes.

3. Man must not be discouraged if he fails to see any improvement in his moral qualities after much self-discipline. Man must train himself so that he no longer obeys the ethical teachings reluctantly but follows them quite naturally.

4. A rabbi they don't want to drive out of town is no rabbi, and a rabbi who lets himself be driven out is no man.

5. Normally, we worry about our own material well-being and our neighbor's soul. Let us rather worry about our neighbor's material well-being and our own souls.

IN SUMMATION

Israel Salanter was one of the most active rabbinic personalities in Lithuania and Russia in the nineteenth century. Clearly, his lasting legacy was his founding of the Musar movement, the setting up of special ethical houses of learning, and the publishing of a journal (Tevunah) to disseminate his ideas. Since its founding, the Musar movement has remained an influential force, especially within the Orthodox Jewish world, affecting the curriculum of many major yeshivot. One of its most famous offshoots is the Navaradok School of Musar, founded by Rabbi Joseph Horowitz of Navaradok, a student of Rabbi Salanter. His ethical works were collected by his pupil Isaac Belzer in *Or Israel*.

22

ZECHARIAH FRANKEL

BACKGROUND

Born in 1801 in Prague, Frankel received a Talmudic education under Bazalel Ronsburg. In 1831 the Austrian government appointed him district rabbi of Leitmeritz, and he settled in Teplitz where he was elected local rabbi. He was the first Bohemian rabbi with a secular academic education and one of the very first to preach in German. In 1836 he was called by the Saxon government to Dresden to act as chief rabbi. In 1854 Frankel became the director of the newly founded Juedisch-Theologisches Seminar at Breslau, where he remained until his death in 1875. In this school he endeavored to combine Jewish religious tradition with the European enlightenment.

RELIGIOUS OUTLOOK

As a theologian, Frankel aimed at a synthesis between the historical conservative conception and contemporary needs, throughout gradual organic reform. Becoming the spiritual leader of the party that advocated "moderate reforms," he founded the "positive-historical" Breslau school, which later influenced the Conservative movement in the United States. Frankel always maintained that only the changes that were not in conflict with the spirit of historical Judaism should be permitted in the traditional ritual. He believed that the messianic belief was of importance for both the survival and the development of Judaism, and that it brought a new spirit and vigor into the life of German Jews.

At the second rabbinic conference at Frankfurt in 1845, Frankel pressed for the formulation of a firm principle as a guide to the adoption of slight additional reforms. The main opponents to his demands were Abraham Geiger and S. Holdheim. In protest against its rejection, and against the proposed gradual abolition of Hebrew as the language of worship, Frankel withdrew from the conference.

WRITINGS

In his scholarly works, Frankel dealt mainly with biblical-Talmudic law, the historical development of Jewish law, and Talmudic exegesis. He saw all the laws as God-given, not necessarily in direct communication, but through the experiences of the Jewish people in its long historical quest of God. His first scholarly work, entitled *Die Eidesleistung bei den Juden* on the Jewish oath, arose out of a practical need and was at the same time a pioneering attempt at scientific analysis of Halakhic problems using the method of comparative jurisprudence. Several of his works deal with the history of oral tradition. In his first study on the Septuagint, *Vorstudien zu der Septuaginta*, Frankel tried to show that traces of the Palestinian *halachah* could be found in the Greek translation of the Bible. He also wrote *Ahavat Ziyyon*, a commentary to several tractates of the Jerusalem Talmud. In 1851 he founded the *Monatsschrift für Geschichte und Wissenschaft des Judenthums*, editing it for seventeen years and publishing numerous articles on Jewish cultural history. In the Breslau seminary, Frankel set the standard for modern rabbinic training. His curriculum of study and the qualifications he established for students and teachers were adopted by similar institutions.

IN SUMMATION

Zechariah Frankel believed in a Judaism that, while it adapted itself to needs of the modern day, remained clearly and distinctly the Jewish religion, with its forms, its own ideas and hopes, its own fellowship with Jews of every land. In all his works, he showed that he was a "critical" student of Jewish tradition, believing that changes could be made in Judaism, but always with moderation and care. He saw Judaism as a historical religion that changes gradually in response to various challenges, but it changes organically, not by violent interruption of Jewish growth and development. The school he founded was always open to modern critical studies on the Bible and Talmud.

His centrist position, between Orthodox and Reform, paved the way for the Conservative branch of Judaism in the United States.

23

THE NEO-KANTIANISM OF HERMANN COHEN

BACKGROUND

Born in 1842 in Coswig, this German philosopher, the son of a cantor, studied at the Jewish Theological Seminary at Breslau. Originally wanting to become a rabbi, he gave up that idea, turning to philosophy. He first studied at the University of Breslau and then at the University of Berlin.

In 1873 he became a lecturer in philosophy at the University of Marburg where he taught until 1912. His early works were devoted primarily to an evaluation of idealism as embodied in the thought of Plato and Kant. These works, which included Kant's *Theory of Experience*, brought Cohen to a new interpretation of Kant's philosophy, which came to be known as the Marburg School of neo-Kantianism. This approach found expression in works entitled *The Logic of Pure Knowledge, The Ethics of the Pure Will,* and *The Aesthetic of Pure Feelings.* These works reflected Cohen's contention that philosophy's three main branches are logic, ethics, and aesthetics, which investigate the underlying assumptions of the basic modes of consciousness: thinking, willing, and feeling, respectively. He died in 1918.

He spent the last years of life in Berlin where he taught at the Hochschule für die Wissenschaft des Judentums.

COHEN'S PHILOSOPHIC SYSTEM

The starting point of Cohen's philosophic system, like that of Kant's, is the existence of scientific knowledge, expressed mathematically. Like Kant, Cohen believed that the philosopher's task is to unfold the logical conditions underlying this type of knowledge.

According to Cohen, thought produces everything out of itself. Thus he opposed Kant's notion of the "thing-in-itself": behind the object that we know there lies an object that can never be known as it really is.

Describing the methodology of science, Cohen holds that the scientist posits certain basic principles that help him to determine the facts, but as research progresses, he is required to revise these underlying principles and to conceive new theories, which in turn lead to the discovery of new facts. In accordance with this view, one's knowledge of reality at any given time is determined by the particular stage of this process. Since the process is unending, a person can never have a final knowledge of reality.

Regarding ethics, Cohen held that the dignity of the human being is central. Thus he regarded a nation's treatment of its working classes as an index of its level of morality.

ETHICS AND THE IDEA OF GOD

Although Cohen had maintained that religion was only a historical presupposition for ethics, and that ethics was destined to absorb religion, the idea of God played a central role in his ethics. For Cohen, ethics provides humankind with an eternal ideal, but natural science indicates that the world is nearing its end. If humankind were to cease to exist, there would be no possibility of achieving the ethical ideal. It is here that Cohen introduces his concept of God, whose function it is to guarantee the eternity of the world, and thus the fulfillment of the moral ideal. Cohen's conception of God was quite different from that of the personal God of traditional Judaism. For Cohen, God was an idea or concept rather than an existent being.

COHEN'S REVOLUTIONARY NEW GOD IDEA

At age 70, when Cohen moved from Marburg to Berlin, his contact with the Jews in Vilna and Warsaw brought marked change in his concept of God. His book *The Concept of Religion Within The Philosophical System*, written in 1915, bears witness to the change. In this volume, Cohen attempted to accord religion an independent place within the philosophic system. Cohen maintained that there are problems that ethics cannot explain. Although ethics is concerned with man in general, it fails to take into account the personal concerns of the individual. Whereas the Early Prophets judged the world from the general ethical standpoint, the Later Prophets (Jeremiah, Isaiah, and Ezekiel) are very concerned with the individual. Cohen identified prophetic Judaism with the highest spiritual insight of the Jewish people and with ethical monotheism (a concept of the God grounding moral responsibility).

Cohen's new attitude found its expression in his work *The Religion of Reason from the Sources of Judaism*, which was published posthumously by his wife. This book clearly shows that Cohen had abandoned his belief that reality is rooted in God with man's reason itself originating in God. For Cohen, God was no longer an idea, but a pure Being while the world was becoming.

Relative to the question that now arises concerning how a world that is becoming could possibly exist beside God who is an eternal being, Cohen develops the new concept of "correlation." Being and becoming are connected to one another insofar as one concept logically requires the other. That is to say, becoming could not exist if there were no eternal existence (i.e., God) who could endow it with power. On the other hand, being could not exist without becoming, and the existence of God would have no meaning without creation.

CORRELATION BETWEEN GOD AND MAN

Cohen maintained that the correlation between God and man is characterized by the holy spirit, *ruach ha-kodesh*, which is not an attribute of either God or man, but of their relation. Cohen criticized Christianity and Philo for positing the holy spirit as an independent being intermediate between God and man, and failing to realize that it is, in his opinion, only an attribute of the relationship between man and God. The holy spirit binds man and God together, and the correlation between man and God is manifest in man's attempt to imitate God, the source of all holiness, and to become holy himself. Man's specific creative mission is to help all people live in peace and harmony, which will bring about the messianic era. Cohen conceived of the messianic era in terms of a philosophic socialism. The struggle of the messianic kingdom was a struggle for justice and the rights of the impoverished. The Jewish people need to serve as the role model of all humanity.

GOD'S COMMANDMENTS

Although Cohen posited a liberal interpretation of Judaism, which emphasized its moral teachings, he vigorously affirmed the value of Jewish tradition and law. Following Immanuel Kant and his doctrine of morality (which maintains that an action is moral if it is performed from a sense of duty and is autonomous), Cohen interprets God's command (i.e., *mitzvah*) to mean both "law" and "duty." The law originates in God while the sense of duty originates in people. God issues commandments to man, and man, of his own free will, takes upon himself the so-called "yoke of the commandments." With the "yoke of the commandments," man simultaneously accepts the "yoke of the kingship of God." Thus, the law leads to the messianic ideal. Cohen rejected Zionism, for he saw in the national conception of Judaism a betrayal of the messianic ideal.

IN SUMMATION

Cohen's influence on other Jewish intellectuals was profound. He argued that within Judaism one finds represented the correct understanding of the dynamic relationship between man and God. This new appraisal of the relation of Judaism to philosophy and Cohen's demand that religion was not to be subordinated to philosophic demands revolutionized Jewish thought. Franz Rosenzweig and Martin Buber were especially influenced by Cohen, particularly his concept of correlation, which became the source of much of the dialogical relationship of God and man. Buber was indebted to Cohen for liberating Jewish thought, allowing Judaism to assert its own independent claims to truth and value.

24

SOLOMON SCHECHTER

BACKGROUND

Born in 1847 in Focsani, Rumania, Solomon Schechter, rabbinic scholar, was the president of the Conservative Movement's Jewish Theological Seminary of America. From 1875 through 1879 he studied at the Vienna *bet hamidrash* where he acquired a devotion to scientific study of the tradition. Soon thereafter he developed the central notion of the community of Israel as the decisive factor for Jewish living and creativity. He was to call it "catholic Israel," implying a universal people. Schechter never fully explained all the ramifications of this imaginative term. Nevertheless, it made a powerful impact on the Jewish community.

In 1890 Schechter was appointed lecturer in Talmud at Cambridge. His identification of a Hebrew fragment brought from Egypt as part of the lost Hebrew original of Ecclesiasticus resulted in his journey in 1896 to 1897 to Cairo, whence he removed the remaining contents of the Genizah to Cambridge.

His remarkably fruitful work on these materials greatly enhanced his reputation, and in 1901 he was appointed president of the Jewish Theological Seminary of America in New York City. Under his direction, this became a scholastic institution of the first rank. He developed the Seminary and its associated organizations, such as the United Synagogue of America (today known as the United Synagogue of Conservative Judaism), as the institutions of Conservative Judaism, the philosophy of which he elaborated in a series of works and addresses.

Schechter served as Honorary President of the United Synagogue until his death in 1915. Besides his editing of important scholarly works, such as *Avot De Rabbi Natan*, he published in English several works combining scholarship with popular appeal, such as *Some Aspects of Rabbinic Theology* and especially *Studies in Judaism* (three volumes).

CATHOLIC ISRAEL

Schechter maintained that one important factor that influenced Jewish law was that of the customs of the people. The decisions of the rabbis and the practices of the community of Israel often coincided, but sometimes they did not. When that happened, the rabbis sometimes attempted to change the practices of the people to fit the law, but sometimes they adjusted the law to fit the customs of the people. For Schechter, Jewish law was always a product of an interaction between the rabbis and the rest of the Jewish people.

Solomon Schechter maintained that Jewish law should be determined by what he called "catholic Israel." Here Schechter is using the term catholic to mean "the whole of," and thus catholic Israel was Schechter's way of defining *klal Yisrael*—the whole of the community of Israel. He used this term to indicate that decisions in Jewish law should be determined by the practices of the whole community of Israel. He thus maintained that liberty was given to the great teachers of every generation to make modifications and innovations that were harmonious with the spirit of the existing institutions. This removed the center of authority from the Bible and placed it in the hands of the whole community of Israel.

THEOLOGY

One of Solomon Schechter's main contributions to Jewish theology was his rediscovery that to be fully understood it must be experienced emotionally. That is to say, it must be felt as well as known. The emotional reactions evoked by concepts such as God's kingdom, the messiah, and revelation are as much a part of the doctrines as the propositions themselves regarding them.

For Schechter, Judaism was a system of conduct rather than mere belief. Thus he was not much attracted to the philosophic efforts of Maimonides, his predecessors, and his followers, since these works were generally based on interpretation and reinterpretation.

Schechter wrote extensively on the concept of *simcha shel mitzvah*—the joy of the law. He maintained that the joy of performing a religious obligation is the essence of action and cited the biblical fact that when Israel stood on Mount Sinai to receive the Torah, they all combined with one heart to accept the kingdom of heaven in joy.

SIN AS REBELLION

Schechter agreed with rabbinic tradition that sin and disobedience ought to be conceived as defiance and rebellion. Sin causes separation between man and God. It was also viewed as a symptom of corruption and decay in the spiritual condition of man. One of the sources of sin is the *yetzer hara*—the evil imagination or inclination that each and every person possesses.

Schechter maintained that the two great passions that the evil inclination plays most upon are the passions of idolatry and adultery.

Finally, Schechter posits that every person has in his or her power the ability to resist the evil inclination. One of the recommended weapons used in the war against the evil inclination is occupation with study of Torah and deeds of kindness. Schechter concludes his discussion of the evil inclination by stating that with the advent of the Messiah, the evil inclination will cease.

IN SUMMATION

Out of the vast expanse of Talmud and Midrash, Solomon Schechter distilled in his writings the principles and dogmas that have been consistent in Jewish life everywhere through the centuries. He is considered the architect of Conservative Judaism in America, having succeeded in creating an organization that is loyal to the Torah and rabbinic tradition but at the same time is able to adopt scientific methods in its training of its students.

The Conservative movement has also sponsored the creation of many Solomon Schechter schools, the largest federation of non-Orthodox day schools in the United States.

25

ABRAHAM ISAAC KOOK

BACKGROUND

Born in 1865 in Greiva Latvia, this rabbinic authority and thinker was the first Ashkenazi chief rabbi of the modern State of Israel. At a young age, he studied Bible, Hebrew language, Jewish and general philosophy, and mysticism. In 1888 he was appointed rabbi of Zaumel and in 1895 he became rabbi of Bausk.

In 1904 he immigrated to Israel where he served as rabbi of Jaffa. He identified with the Zionist movement and urged traditional Jews to fulfill the Zionist ideal by traveling to Europe in 1914 to participate in a conference of Agudat Israel. Unable to return to Israel because of the outbreak of World War I, Kook accepted a temporary position as rabbi of the Machzikei ha-Dat congregation in London. Upon returning to Palestine after the war, he was appointed chief rabbi of Jerusalem, and with the formation of the chief rabbinate in 1921, he was elected the first Ashkenazi chief rabbi of Palestine.

In 1924 he set up a yeshivah in Jerusalem that was unique

among yeshivot in its religious philosophy and its positive attitude to Zionism. This yeshivah became known as Merkaz ha-Rav.

KOOK'S MYSTICISM

Kook is a fine example of a twentieth-century phenomenon: the deeply religious mystic who is extremely interested in human affairs. Kook's mystical system blends mystical speculation and practical activities. Most mystical systems insist that man remove himself of the restraints of physical life in order to achieve mystical union with God. In Kook's system, however, the mystical urge for unity was meant to combine the communicable with the mysterious—to infuse the physical life of man with a religious purpose. There was no stress on self-denial in his system.

Throughout his life Kook carried on a relentless search for the meaning of religion in the modern world. In his opinion, Zionism was a movement of rebellion, which attracted Jewish intellectuals who had abandoned their religious faith. Kook believed in a movement of return to the national homeland that would be a religious one, for it was only in the land of Israel that the Jewish people could express a complete religious life.

SOCIAL PHILOSOPHY

While Kook was critical of social ideologies that limited their interest to material conditions only, he at the same time criticized religious people who were not interested in social issues related to improving the world. He was especially troubled by society's preoccupation with the acquisition of wealth and maintained that a consistent application of Torah laws in social and economic matters would never tolerate the prevailing capitalist system. Kook interpreted the biblical Jubilee year (Leviticus 25:8–12) as a suspension of all acquisitive economic dealings. In that year equality and tranquility would manifest themselves, and there would be neither master nor oppressor, no private property, and no special privileges.

Kook's social philosophy was rooted in his theory of the relationship of religious piety to morality. For Kook, the criterion of pure piety is that the natural morality, which is inherent in man's nature, steadily improve over and above what it would have been without his piety.

CURRENT CHALLENGES TO RELIGION

Kook believed that the twentieth century saw incredible progress in everything in the world except religion. He identified three elements that led to man's unhappiness with religion: (1) man's new perception of human society involved an outlook that believed in a more universal view of the world; (2) the scientific picture of the universe was not in harmony with the traditional religious view; and (3) the theory of evolution upset the established patterns of religious thought.

Kook also posited that in the eyes of twentieth-century man, religion seemed to be indifferent to social issues. He was convinced, however, that the irreligion of man would eventually pass, and heightened spirituality would be realized, having only been hidden in social passion.

THE JEWS AS CHOSEN PEOPLE

For Kook, Jewish nationality is marked by the concept of chosenness. The Jewish people had a divine mission, namely to perfect humanity. It was up to the Jews as a nation to accept upon themselves their mission and carry out their divine task.

Jewish nationality differs from that of other nations in that its mainspring is not social or economic but divine. For Kook, the divine connection between the people of Israel and the land of

Israel is not the result of historical causes. On the contrary, the connection is the cause of the history of the people of Israel. According to Kook, it was God's plan that led the Israelite people to make the land of Israel its country and to create history there. Thus, according to Kook, both the people of Israel and the land of Israel are holy and sanctified.

IN SUMMATION

In modern Jewish history, there have been few Orthodox rabbis as deeply beloved by non-Orthodox Jews as Rabbi Abraham Isaac Kook. As preeminent hero of religious Zionists, Kook also felt an enormous kinship with all Jews involved in their pioneering efforts to settle and build the land of Israel. Kook also saw value in secular education, unlike many Orthodox rabbis whose curriculum was only religious in nature.

Kook was also a prolific writer, whose works continue to be read and studied. His speculative writings are contained in his *Orot HaKodesh* (three volumes) and *Orot HaTeshuvah*. His Halakhic works include *Shabbat Haaretz* and *Da'at Kohen*.

26

LEO BAECK

BACKGROUND

Born in 1873, Baeck was a German rabbi and leader of the movement of Progressive Judaism. He first studied at the Conservative Jewish Theological Seminary of Breslau and later at the Liberal Hochschule für die Wissenschaft des Judentums in Berlin. At the same time he also studied philosophy at the University of Breslau.

From 1933 Baeck was president of the Reichsvertretung, the representative body of German Jews, and devoted himself to defending the rights remaining for Jews under the Nazis.

At the Theresienstadt concentration camp, to which he was deported in 1943, he was named honorary president of the Aeltestenrat and continued the work of encouraging the people. In 1945, after the war was over, he moved to London where he became president of the Council of Jews from Germany and chairman of the World Union for Progressive Judaism.

Baeck's works include *Wege im Judentum*, a collection of

essays and speeches; *Aus drei Jahrtausenden*, a collection of scholarly papers; and *Judaism and Christianity*. His minor work was entitled *Wesen des Judentums (The Essence of Judaism)*, which over the years has appeared in numerous translations. From 1948 until his death he taught in the United States as professor of the history of religion at Hebrew Union College in Cincinnati.

NATURE OF GOD

Baeck was a philosophic thinker of wide general knowledge. He drew heavily on the Jewish thought of Hermann Cohen. As opposed to Cohen, however, Baeck argues that the idea of God has little more religious value than any other pure idea. The certainty that God is real does not derive from a rational demonstration that God is the First Cause in the universe, but rather in what has happened in peoples' lives, in the sense of meaning and direction that they have. For Baeck, God is not to be understood as a God of qualities or about whom dogmas may be listed. However, Judaism is well aware that since people are conscious of God as One who is responsive to people, God can be understood personally and regarded as personal.

Baeck further maintains that there is a fundamental paradox about God as presented in Judaism. On the one hand, God is a transcendent God—exalted and Sovereign King. On the other hand, God is a personal God—Our Father and Parent. Thus the ethical and the devotional are simultaneously affirmed in Judaism. God can be personally sensed but still retains His quality of being an ethically demanding God.

MYSTERIES AND COMMANDMENTS

Baeck viewed the essence of Judaism as a dialectical polarity between "mystery" and "command." The commands, according to Baeck, do not necessarily form a system of commandments like the established *halachah* (system of Jewish law), which imposes a fixed and very directed way of life. Rather, they appear from time to time in the form of instructions for action like lightning bolts that break through the clouds covering the Divine "mystery." Baeck continued to adhere to Hermann Cohen's interpretation of Judaism as "ethical monotheism." He believed that the piety is achieved by the fulfillment of the duties between man and man, and that even observances through ritual are directed toward this ethical aim.

ESSENCE OF JUDAISM

Baeck's exposition of the essence of Judaism consists of two basic motifs: human ethics and religious consciousness. One of his central ideas is that human beings have an elemental sense of being created, and yet they also know that they are most true to themselves when they are creators, which is when they act ethically.

For Baeck, ethics, without a grounding in God, is mere moralism. Baeck maintained that for Judaism, there can be no ethics that does not stem from a living God who establishes relationships with humankind.

Judaism, Baeck posits, cannot base itself on unbridled feeling. Rather, Baeck insists, its religious consciousness receives authentic expression only in ethical acts. However, when feeling is channeled into the ethical realm, it often can bring strength to the ethical. This dialectical tension between religious consciousness and ethics is Baeck's unique intellectual creation.

GOOD AND EVIL

Baeck was the only major modern Jewish theologian to enter and survive the death camps. With regard to his theory of evil,

Baeck maintains that the source of evil is the misuse of human freedom. People are responsible for creating evil in the world, and not God. However, people who have committed wrongs can and often do change their ways and make themselves once again acceptable to God. They do this through repentance (*teshuvah*, in Hebrew). For Baeck, people must always take responsibility for what they do. Thus the power to do good or evil is in the hands of humankind.

CHRISTIANITY AND ZIONISM

Baeck sharply rejected Christianity and had a critical attitude toward Zionism. In Christianity he saw a "romantic" religion of the abstract spirit longing for redemption as distinguished from Judaism, the "classical" religion of the concrete spirit working for the improvement of the world. Although not a political Zionist, Baeck thought that the building of Palestine was a valuable prospect for embodying the spirit of Judaism, but not a guarantee that it would be realized. This he maintained could succeed wherever there is a Jewish community that truly deserves it.

IN SUMMATION

Baeck is considered one of the leading spiritual figures of modern liberal Judaism. The World Union of Progressive Judaism was established at his initiative. There has been lasting greatness to Baeck's thought, especially in his reaffirming the right of religion to speak to the heart. Although reason and rationalism appealed to so many Jews of the time, Baeck persisted in upholding his belief that personal spirituality was always to be a part of the essence of Judaism.

27

FRANZ ROSENZWEIG

BACKGROUND

This German Jewish philosopher was born in Kassel in 1886. Born of an assimilated family, he was on the point of embracing Christianity when the experience of a traditional Day of Atonement service in 1913 brought him back to Judaism. To the teaching of this he now devoted his whole life. To intensify his knowledge of Judaism, he went to Berlin where he fell under the spell of Hermann Cohen, then teaching at the liberal rabbinic seminary. Here he also made his first acquaintance with Martin Buber, who became his close friend and colleague.

During World War I he was drafted into the German Army and spent part of the war in Poland. He utilized this opportunity to meet with Jews in Warsaw and was very much struck by their piety. As a soldier during World War I, Rosenzweig wrote essays about the needed reforms in general as well as Jewish education. Throughout the war he sent home postcards and letters filled with theological reflections. These became the basis for his most famous book *Der Stern der Erloesung* (*Star of Redemption*). In this volume Rosenzweig sought to demonstrate what existence says about God, the world, and the human species, as well as how the relationships are drawn among them.

After World War I, Rosenzweig moved to Frankfurt on the Main where he organized the Frankfurt Lehrhaus, an innovative Jewish Free University where college-age students and adults, regardless of their qualifications, could register for courses on Judaism, Jewish history, and Hebrew. The goal of the school was to promote Jewish literacy and to encourage Jewish involvement. The Lehrhaus did not advocate any one philosophic or denominational view of Judaism. In the United States today, Rosenzweig's program has served as the model for many Jewish adult educational programs of learning.

In 1921 progressive paralysis completely immobilized Rosenzweig, confining him to his home. There he lived for seven years, continuing his intellectual and literary activities. The main literary products of these years are translations from Hebrew into German. For example, Rosenzweig's translations of Judah Halevi's liturgical poems into German were also accompanied by footnotes that discussed the theological subject matter of the poems.

In 1924 both Rosenzweig and Buber began a new translation of the Bible. The translation was noteworthy because it attempted to reproduce in German what the translators believed to be the originally intended and traditionally preserved oral quality of the biblical texts. By the time of Rosenzweig's death in 1929, they had reached the Book of Isaiah. (Buber completed the project in Israel in the 1950s.)

In general, Rosenzweig's views of the Bible must be regarded as "post-critical." Fully conversant with so-called Bible criticism, he held that the prominent question to be asked about the Bible is not concerned with its origins but with its fate, not what the biblical authors had in mind but what the reader gets out of it.

STAR OF REDEMPTION

Rosenzweig's major work, *The Star of Redemption*, proposes to offer a philosophic theology of both Judaism and Christianity. The three parts of this work can be summarized as follows:

Book 1: Man, the Universe, and God

Rosenzweig regards the world as consisting of three elements: man, the universe, and God. He rejects philosophy's attempt to reduce these three elements to one basic element on the grounds that this does not conform to reality. While in the "pagan" worldview these three elements are independent, according to the biblical view they interact through the processes of creation, revelation, and redemption. According to Rosenzweig, revelation is initiated by God as the process of relating, first God to man, and then man to God, and through his life to the world. Rosenzweig maintains that truth is subjective, is arrived at by the individual on the basis of his own personal existence, and can be verified only in the life of the individual.

Book 2: Revelation of God

For Rosenzweig, revelation is not a single historical event (such as that which occurred atop Mount Sinai), but rather the continuous entry into relationship with man on the part of God. All religions are built on a revelatory experience. Revelation takes a verbal form, and its content is simply God's identification of Himself to people in love. This divine love evokes in turn a response of love in man, which is expressed also in man's relationships with his neighbor. (The three "pagan" elements comprise one triangle, their revelatory relations another, and when superimposed one upon the other they form the "star of redemption.")

Rosenzweig distinguishes between laws that are universal and commandments that are personal. Though revelation does not comprise laws, commandments are born out of the love relationship. When carried out, these commandments change life.

For Rosenzweig, the total content of God's revelation is God's self-disclosure, the fact of His presence and His concern for the Jewish people. By virtue of God's relation to people, God is involved in time and works in history. Thus, Rosenzweig's God is a personal God, very much like the one described in the Bible.

Rosenzweig parts company from his colleague Martin Buber when it comes to understanding the relationship between revelation and Jewish law. Although both agree that law is not part of the content of revelation, Rosenzweig maintains that the sense of "being commanded" is part of revelation's content.

Book 3: Search for the Kingdom of God

Rosenzweig asserts that man's desire in prayer, action, and hope for the permanent reality of the revelatory experience in community is the search for the kingdom of God. The people of Israel entered into this kingdom of eternity from the outset. The Jew is naturally born a Jew, and the continuity of the Jewish people is biological. Thus biology is a theological value. The Jew lives eternity essentially through the religious calendar and liturgy.

Rosenzweig maintains that it is the risky business of Christianity to carry its own members and the rest of humanity toward the consummation in which God will be "all in all." Christians are thus always converts to Christianity, which is superimposed upon their pagan origin. Judaism and Christianity are both partial truths in history, and both will, in the opinion of Rosenzweig, be superseded by the absolute truth in the "end of days."

IN SUMMATION

Rosenzweig's writings and thoughts have exerted a significant influence. One reason for this is that people who were associated with him (including A. J. Heschel, Ignaz Maybaum, and Nahum Glatzer) and who long survived him carried his imprint through their own careers. Another is the fact that in different ways, the problems that Rosenzweig faced in his generation still persist in the late twentieth century: the recovery of Jewish literacy, the relationship between Judaism and Christianity, and the relationship between the secular environment and the Jewish religion.

In 1966 *Commentary* magazine sponsored a symposium of American rabbis on "The State of Jewish Belief." It was noted at this symposium that Rosenzweig was the most often cited influence on the Reform and Conservative participants. A likely reason for this was his openness to the entire Jewish tradition, which he achieved by not identifying with any one particular branch of Judaism. Rosenzweig has also been the guide for many an assimilated Jew who wished to return to a full Jewish life, as did Rosenzweig himself.

To this day, Rosenzweig's thought stands on its own as a special example of Jewish existentialism.

28

MARTIN BUBER AND HIS DIALOGICAL PHILOSOPHY

THE MAN AND HIS CULTURE

Martin Buber's life was a rich tapestry of conditions and events that parallel historical movements and ideological schools of thought. Buber was a product of two great cultures, European (especially German) and Jewish. His intellectual life was affected by the Jewish and the European aspirations and agonies of the last quarter of the nineteenth century and the first half of the twentieth century. Those were turbulent years that were reflected in the optimistic enlightenment of the European culture, the intellectual erudity of the Haskalah, the mystic spirit of the Hasidim, the critical analysis of the German philosophers, the melancholy of two world wars, and the messianic hopes that arose with the establishment of the State of Israel. These movements and thoughts left on his soul indelible intellectual marks. Gradually these impressions blended together and consequently emerged as his unique dialogical philosophy. His philosophic genesis was rooted in his particular Jewish traditional heritage; from here he ventured out into the riches of the secular intellectual world and finally came to rest on his people's universal messianic values. His life and thoughts were intensely interrelated. This interrelationship calls for a study of Buber as a person.

Buber was born in Vienna in 1878. At the age of 3 the boy's parents became estranged and he went to live in Poland with his grandfather, Solomon Buber, a noted scholar of the Haskalah, the Jewish enlightenment movement. In this home he received a solid grounding in traditional Jewish education. He was exposed to the teachings of the two great Jewish movements of that period: the Haskalah and the Hasidut, which influenced his future life immeasurably.

HASIDUT

Both the Hasidic and the Haskalah movements were products of their times and circumstances. They came to answer the needs of their epochs. They brought solace to yearning hearts and meaning to anguished souls.

Sixteenth-century Poland was one of the largest countries in Europe, but two centuries later it was reduced to a vulnerable state that was slated to death. The country drifted to political chaos and economic bankruptcy. Polish Jews, who in the sixteenth century had been the elite of world Jewry, declined by the eighteenth century in strength and stature. In the middle of the seventeenth century, Bodgen Chmielnicki, with his insurrectionist Ukraine army, swept Poland and murdered tens of thousands of Jews. Soon after the devastating rule of the Saxon kings ensued. Their wrath was shrewdly vented against the Jews, resulting in pogroms and massacres.

The latter half of the eighteenth century brought political, economic, and cultural disaster to Poland. In 1792 the troops of

Russia and Prussia moved into Poland, Lithuania, and the Ukraine. Prussia annexed greater Poland, and Russia expropriated substantial parts of Lithuania and the Ukraine. The Polish government became paralyzed, and the lives of the Jews were reduced to the status of pariahs. With their political and economic security having collapsed, they turned to their ancient religion for solace and comfort. Traditional theologies and liturgies could not give them the spiritual comfort they so needed. These were too sophisticated and rational to be of any assistance, and they lacked the ethical significance that Judaism so desperately needed. As an antidote to the melancholy that overtook Jewish life, a new movement—Hasidut—emerged.

Martin Buber came to know Hasidut, the movement that so greatly influenced his later development while he stayed at his grandfather's house. Hasidism was established in the eighteenth century by the afflicted Jews who, in their despair, awaited the coming of the Messiah but instead saw the coming of the Cossack, pogroms, and persecutions. It was a movement that advocated complete confidence in God and realization that God's presence is everywhere. If God is always present, the Hasidim reasoned, why be afraid? Consequently a person should always be joyous. Human beings need only fulfill God's commandments with joy and devotion and they will find their realization.

Even if a person is not learned and even when a person errs out of ignorance or weakness, that person's prayer is accepted because God values inner spirit and good intentions. Like many of the Christian evangelical sects, they emphasized new birth, illumination, animation, song, and inner emotionalism. It was a religion of emotions and feelings, an innovated religion that spoke to the heart. It believed in spiritual healing through prayer and divine thoughts. Being poor and ignorant, the Hasidim professed contempt for intellectualism, positing that one could find fulfillment only in the world of the spirit. In the spiritual world, all are equal: rich and poor, literate and illiterate. Although Buber's early encounter with the Hasidic movement could not win him over completely, he later returned to it as a model and a source of inspiration. The influence of this movement, which emphasized joyful worship of God, impressed him for life. Its impact on him was so great that he withdrew in 1904 from his active life to study their teachings, which he later published in his famous book *The Tales of the Hasidim*.

HASKALAH

During his childhood, Buber encountered yet another great movement that affected his life considerably. This was a movement of scholarship, modernism, and enlightenment, one that returned to the Jew the sense of self-esteem, dignity, and freedom. To this program of Jewish Enlightenment was assigned the name Haskalah.

Throughout the history of humankind, small groups of very influential individuals have shaped and altered the course of human affairs, such as the artists of the Italian Renaissance and the philosophers of eighteenth-century France. In the nineteenth century such a minority made its appearance among the Jews of Eastern Europe and established the Haskalah, the period of Jewish Enlightenment. It revolutionized and modernized Jewish thought and behavior and served as a turning point in Jewish history.

The Maskilim, the Haskalah scholars, vigorously embarked on the path of humanism, scholarship, and emancipation. They urged their fellow Jews to integrate into the secular world community while holding on steadfast to their Jewish tenets and principles. The spirit of the Haskalah quest for knowledge left a lasting mark on Buber. Together with the Hasidic zeal and fervor, it later culminated in his social humanistic concerns and his prophetic universal hopes.

SECULAR INTELLECTUALISM

At the age of 14, Buber left his grandfather's home to study at the gymnasium of Lemberg and the universities of Berlin and Vienna. Western Europe of that era was permeated with new cultural and intellectual currents, and Buber ventured into this world in search of knowledge and direction. Soon he became disenchanted, for the conventional European philosophies did not touch his soul. The only movement that truly affected him and transformed him into a universalist and humanist was the relatively new school of thought and approach to life called existential philosophy. Especially notable was the existentialist school of Soren Kierkegaard, the great Danish theologian, which stressed the significance of personal existence against abstract philosophy. This provided Jewish thinkers, such as Martin Buber, with a different vantage point from which to view the relation between philosophy and religion. From Kierkegaard Buber learned that every person must seek his own pathway to God, and that building faith in God on sheer historical grounds is fatal delusion. Faith can never be expressed purely on philosophic lines and is not expressed in dogma. Buber also learned from Kirkegaard that a person's cherished possession is freedom and that a person's freedom involves a life of toil and much potential danger.

Existential philosophers also maintained that man need not go far to search for solutions to problems such as human suffering in the world. They claimed that the solution lies within man himself. Man need not look for purpose in the universe, because the universe has no purpose. It is only man who has purpose, and the meaning for man's life is to be found within man himself. So it is also with truth, which is not absolute and does not reside outside of man. Truth can only be found within man himself, in his soul.

I AND THOU

Among Buber's books is one entitled *I-Thou*. It is in this book that Buber presents his entire philosophy.

Buber's philosophy is built on the concept of unity. Man's greatest achievement in life, he claims, is the attainment of unity: unity within the single man, unity between man and man, unity among the segments of a nation, unity among nations, unity between humankind and the inanimate world, and unity between the universe and God. This unity is basically spiritual in nature and is achieved by building spiritual bridges between man and man, between man and nature, and between man and his spiritual world. Buber proposes his "I–Thou" dialogue as an instrument for the attainment of this unity.

The world is bipolar. Every subject, according to Buber, is a subject in relationship to a subject. There is no subject without an object and there is no object without a subject. It is the relationship between the two that makes the subject and object what they are. Thus, what really exists between man and man, man and nature, and a man and his spiritual world is a relationship, or more correctly an attitude.

Buber spoke of two primary attitudes between man and his surrounding world: the "I–Thou" and the "I–It" attitudes. The basic words "I," "Thou," and "It," he explained, come in pairs, in which the two words relate to each other. The word "I" does not exist by itself nor do the words "Thou" and "It." They are intertwined into an "I–Thou" or an "I–It" relationship. In order to accentuate the special meaning of these relationships, Buber deliberately ignored the common word "you" and instead used the word "Thou," which represents in his vocabulary uniqueness and importance. By using the word "Thou," he wished to connote presentness, mutuality, directness, familiarity, and ineffability. He wished to connote the familiarity, mutuality, and inclusiveness that exist between a living mother and her beloved child, between husband and wife in the passion of merged feelings and understanding, where the common word "you" does not suffice. The personal familiar "Thou" is required to indicate a binding relationship and an attitude of communion. The "I–Thou" attitude is required to indicate a binding relationship and an attitude of communion. The "I–Thou" attitude represents the highest level of relationship, which is exemplified through authentic communion and loss of consciousness.

While "I-Thou" is dialogue, "I-It" is monologue. "I-It" is one-sided, relating to man's confined physical and empirical world, to the world of things, to the world of use and experience. The "I-It" is a subject–object relationship. It is an attitude that is always indirect, treating even people as objects. This is a theory void of mutuality and communion.

The world that is composed of an "I–It" philosophy is totally different from the world that is founded on an "I–Thou" relationship. The world of the "I-It " is a world where man exists at the side of objects and where one object exists at the side of another object. A table, a chair, a pencil, an eraser, and even a messenger boy who happens to pass through an office are no more than things that happen to exist side by side without interrelationship and without mutuality with the person who happens to occupy the office. Theirs is a mere "I–It" relationship and no more.

Not so with the mother who firmly clasps in her shaking hands the picture of her beloved son who is always away at war, or the frightened little girl who clutches in her hands her cherished rag doll and stares straight into its glass eyes begging for protection and comfort. In these cases, the picture is not an image and the rag doll is indeed not an object. Both exist and are vividly alive in the eyes of their beholders. The picture and the doll are both "Thou" incarnate, responding to those who address them.

Buber further explains that while the "It" need not become a "Thou" at all, the "Thou" cannot forever remain a "Thou", no matter how exclusively present the "Thou" is in the direct relationship. "I" maintains with "Thou" only fleeting glances. The

"Thou" continually becomes an "It" and the "It" may only occasionally become a "Thou" again. Buber presents an example of such a relationship between the "I" and "Thou:" A child, lying in its bed with half-closed eyes, waits with a tense soul for its mother to speak to it, anxiously desiring to communicate with her. The mother arrives, they glance at each other, their eyes shining with love. This to Buber is an experience of communion and mutuality. But the experience is short-lived, for soon the same child views its mother just like any other object. Now the child calls her no more and neither does the mother answer. The "Thou" has been replaced by the "It."

Man can choose to live entirely in the world of "It," but the consequence of this choice is that man loses his humanity.

Buber explained that the "I–Thou" relationship exists in all realms of life, including those of nature and people.

BETWEEN MAN AND NATURE

Buber's autobiography relates an example of a dialogue with nature. He tells of spending a summer vacation on his grandfather's estate, stealing into the stable, and gently stroking the neck of a gray horse. The horse, when Buber began pouring oats for it, raised its massive head and then snorted quietly, indicating its approval. Buber had encountered an "I–Thou" relationship with the horse. He goes on to describe how the beautiful "I–Thou" relationship with the horse ceased when once, while stroking the animal, he felt the fun this motion gave him. It was as though he were using and taking advantage of the horse for his own benefit, and instantly his beloved "Thou" became an "It."

BETWEEN MAN AND MAN

We have seen how an object of nature—a horse—could be treated as a "Thou" with an attitude of communion and inclusion. But just as a man could treat a horse as a "Thou," so too is it possible for a person to treat another person as an object, an "It." Buber describes a doctor–patient relationship as a case in point. A doctor who projects himself into his patient with concern and affection, and feels his pain and sorrow, says "Thou" to his patient, but when the same doctor treats a patient as a "case" among many other cases, he regards him no more than an "It." It is the different attitudes of the doctor to his two patients that Buber refers to as the "in between." In the final analysis, what determines human relations is the attitude between man and man.

GOD, THE ETERNAL THOU

Buber's analysis of the "I–Thou" relation leads him to his notion of God as the Eternal Thou and to his description of the relation between man and God as an "I–Thou" relation. God, the Eternal Thou, is known not through cognitive propositions or through metaphysical speculation but through one's particular "I–Thou" relationships with persons, animals, and nature. The meetings with the Eternal Thou constitute revelation. Thus, for Buber, revelation is not only something that happened many years ago at Mount Sinai, but something that happens in the present, through a person's life. For Buber, the Bible itself is simply a record of the dialogical encounters between man and God. Since the laws of the Bible are only the human response to revelation, they are therefore not binding on later generations.

The dialogue between God and the Israelites is epitomized in the covenant, which lies at the basis of Jewish messianism. God, Buber asserts, demands that the Israelites become a holy people, thereby making the real sovereignty of God in every aspect of communal life. For Buber, the essence of the religious life is not one's affirmation of religious belief, but the way in which one meets the challenges of everyday life.

BUBER AND EVIL

Buber asserted that the failure to enter into a genuine dialogue constitutes evil, whereas the reestablishment of the dialogue can defeat the evil. For Buber, a relationship that is exclusively of an "I–It" nature is evil.

Buber posited two stages of evil. In stage one, a person remains passive, inert, and inactive, allowing things to happen rather than using freedom of choice to act. The second stage is the actual decision to do evil.

Later in his life, as his response to the evil perpetrated in the Holocaust, Buber posited the notion of what he called "radical evil." This idea asserts that there are extraordinary times (such as those of the Holocaust) when God withdraws His presence from humanity. This philosophic-theological concept has come to be known as "hiding of God's face" (*hester panim* in Hebrew), the eclipse and silence of God. Buber leaves unanswered the question of whether one can believe in a God who at times withdraws.

BUBER AND HUMANISTIC EDUCATION

At the Third International Pedagogical Conference held in Heidelberg, Germany in 1925, Buber delivered an address on education. This talk and Buber's subsequent addresses were received by educators with great enthusiasm because a bridge that never existed before, that between existentialism and education, was spanned. This was the first time that an existential philosopher treated education as a serious topic for philosophic inquiry.

Buber established an extensive existential philosophy of education, which naturally corresponded to his "I–Thou" dialogic philosophy. Some have said that his unique educational existential philosophy was the ideological blueprint of the authentic modern open school.

For Buber, a good educator sees his or her fellow students as a "Thou." Communion, authentic human relationship, is the kernel of education, and its process is dialogue. According to Buber, learning is continuous and coincidental. The whole environment—nature and society, the home, the street, music, science—teaches human beings both by mere contact and by indirect action. Genuine education, on the other hand, must be purposeful, understandingly executed by the teacher. If education is to take place, there cannot be a mutual relationship between the teacher and his pupil. Only the teacher may experience his pupil being educated, but the pupil must not experience the educating of his teacher. For Buber, should a mutual relationship arise between student and teacher, education can no longer take place, for now the teacher and his student will have entered into the relationship of friendship, and such a relationship robs the teacher of his strength to select the effective world of his student.

Following are ten of Buber's assertions related to his philosophy of education:

1. Teaching is inseparable from deed. Learning is useless without living, and the pure amassing of knowledge is not education. It must lead to deeds.

2. The education of character is the supreme goal of the educational endeavor.

3. The teacher's only access to the totality of his student is to win his confidence.

4. A major task of education is to awaken in students the desire to assume responsibility for their actions.

5. Adult education is very important. Ordinary teachers, Buber asserted, would not qualify as teachers of adults. (In 1949 Buber founded the Teacher's Institute for the Education of Adults.)

6. The teaching of values is important. Buber's most cherished values were those inherent in the *Five Books of Moses* and Books of the Prophets.

7. Genuine education aspires to educate students so that their acquired knowledge becomes an organic part of their whole life.

8. Good teachers exert their influence not by what they teach but through their teaching personality.

9. Teachers ought not to dictate to students but should permit them to reach their own conclusions.

10. Genuine education is not achieved through prescription but by example. What counts in education more than content and educational strategy is the quality, integrity, sincerity, and commitment of the teacher, his identity with his students, and his ability to see the world from the student's point of view.

IN SUMMATION

Buber introduced a new way of thinking about relating to others. His "I–Thou" philosophy has had a strong influence on modern Jewish educators. He not only viewed education from an existential viewpoint, but established an extensive existential philosophy of education that corresponds to his "I–Thou" dialogic philosophy. Buber emphasized the spiritual qualities of the teacher: personality, commitment to scholarship, and empathy with students and their needs. He also proposed a curriculum based on his "I–Thou" philosophic theory that would teach students to transcend their selves and their national welfare and to learn to integrate themselves with their families, their immediate society, their nation, and with humankind at large.

29

MORDECAI KAPLAN: JUDAISM AS A CIVILIZATION

BACKGROUND

Mordecai Kaplan was born in Lithuania and emigrated to the United States at 9 years of age. Raised in an Orthodox home, he began to grapple with more radical conceptions of the Bible and Judaism.

After his ordination at the Jewish Theological Seminary of America, school of the Conservative branch of Judaism, he became rabbi of the Orthodox synagogue Kehillat Jeshurun in New York City.

In 1909 Solomon Schechter, president of the Jewish Theological Seminary, appointed Kaplan dean of the Teacher's Institute. Soon thereafter Kaplan's teaching included homiletics, Midrash, and religious philosophy.

In 1922 Kaplan founded the Society for the Advancement of Judaism, which later became the Jewish Reconstructionist Foundation (1935). In the same year that the Society for the Advancement of Judaism was founded, Kaplan's daughter Judith became America's first *bat mitzvah*.

Kaplan taught at the Jewish Theological Seminary for five decades and influenced scores of rabbis. As a student of the history of Jewish thought, Kaplan has made significant contributions. He edited and translated *Mesillat Yesharim* by Moses Chayim Luzzatto, contributed a study of Hermann Cohen's philosophy, *The Meaning and Purpose of Jewish Existence* (1964), and described modern Jewish ideologies in *The Greater Judaism in the Making*. Other works include *Judaism as a Civilization, The Meaning of God in Modern Jewish Religion,* and *Questions Jews Ask*.

Kaplan also developed the idea of *chavurot*, small Jewish groups that would get together for study and observance of life-cycle events. This idea later evolved into the *chavurah* movement of today.

Upon Kaplan's departure from the Jewish Theological Seminary, his followers began to organize Reconstructionism as a separate movement with synagogues and its own rabbinic association. In 1968, The Reconstructionist Rabbinical College (RCC) was founded in Philadelphia. Today, the flagship synagogue of the Reconstructionist movement is the Society for the Advancement of Judaism (founded by Kaplan), located in New York City.

The Reconstructionist movement of today continues to grow, and several of Kaplan's most fundamental teachings (e.g., the rejection of the Jews as the chosen and the rejection of a transcendent personal God) are found to be unacceptable to some Reconstructionist rabbis and rabbinic students.

Kaplan died at age 102 in 1983. Among his legacies was surely the founding of what is today a fourth branch of Judaism: Reconstructionism.

JUDAISM AS A CIVILIZATION

The magnum opus of Kaplan, in which he articulates the philosophy of Reconstructionism and the foundational principle that Judaism is more than a religion, is the volume *Judaism As A Civilization*. Kaplan called Judaism an "evolving religious civilization" that encompasses religion, language, history, a social organization, standard of conduct, and spiritual and ethical ideals. He maintained that the preservation of Judaism required that the Jewish people identify with all of the aforementioned aspects of their ancient civilization. He further asserted that in each aspect of civilization, radical adjustments in Jewish social theory and policy are essential. Therefore, while Kaplan has been a devout Zionist, he has also insisted that the creative survival of the Jewish people in the Diaspora is both possible and desirable.

Kaplan also held that Jewish civilization expresses its genius best in clarifying the purposes and values of human existence, in wrestling with God (conceived in nonpersonal terms), and in the ritual of home, synagogue, and community. However, because Judaism is a civilization, the secular elements of culture are essential to Jewish spirituality, curbing the tendency of religion toward rigidity and uniformity.

Kaplan also maintained that Judaism should be considered from a practical, historical point of view, rather than a metaphysical revelational one. Thus, the focus of the content of Jewish life is the Jewish people and its needs, rather than revealed texts. Kaplan also argues that the Jewish people will not accept a static view of Judaism. Each Jew by himself or herself must solve life's perplexities on his or her own. Tradition can be a guide but never a dictator.

KAPLAN'S NATURALISM

For Kaplan, modern science rendered untenable the concept of a personal God who intervenes in human history and knows the mind of each individual. Kaplan believed in the doctrine of godliness, that inside each human being is a spirit that serves as one's moral guide. Kaplan's naturalistic God concept is based on the proposition that the world can be explained in scientifically verifiable ideas. Both in the past and even in modern times, Kaplan asserts, many people consider God a supernatural Being who operated outside the bounds of natural law. Today, Kaplan asserts, people are more sophisticated and have difficulty considering the establishment of a relationship with the supernatural. Kaplan's religious naturalism (the denial of supernaturalistic events) challenges the belief in historical revelation and theologies related to the metaphysical, supernatural interpretations of revelation. He argues that the idea of God is correlative to the idea of man and that conceptions of God necessarily bear an organic relationship to a person's understanding of oneself and the world. Thus, Kaplan regards God as that power in the universe on which man must rely for the achievement of his destiny. The implication of such a definition of God is that God-ideas will reflect advances in the physical and normative sciences. In addition, whenever people display moral responsibility, they are manifesting the presence of God. To the extent that people strive to know the moral law and live up to it, we achieve, in Kaplan's words, "salvation" or "self-realization."

IMPLICATIONS OF KAPLAN'S THEOLOGY

Since God is not a Personal Commander, he understood the so-called divine commandments (i.e., *mitzvot*) as "folkways" of the Jewish people. Kaplan's rejection of a personal deity also forced him to reject the traditional chosen people doctrine as well. Without a personal God, the Jews obviously could not have been chosen. Kaplan also felt that it was arrogant for Jews to assert that God had singled them out among the nations for a special mission. In dropping the idea of chosenness, Kaplan introduced into the Reconstructionist prayer book a controversial change to the blessing for the Torah *aliyah*. In the traditional blessings, Jews thank God for "having chosen them from among all the nations." In Kaplan's prayer book, the Torah blessing reads for "having brought us nigh to Thy service."

The concept of a nonpersonal God advanced by Kaplan also precludes the concept of miracles and the suspension of natural law.

Finally, if God is a Process and not a personal God, what is the meaning of prayer, and can God hear our prayers? In Kaplan's philosophy, prayer takes on a new meaning. Kaplan maintains that people do not pray to a Process, but they can call their attention to the Process. For Kaplan, it is not important if one's prayers are actually heard. What is significant is a person "voicing" his or her yearnings for the achievement of all the goals that in their totality spell God. Thus, for Kaplan, one should not expect one's prayers alone to alter natural events in the world. Prayer is, rather, an incentive program for action and a chance to express one's own wishes.

Finally for Kaplan, evil is that aspect of life that hinders self-realization (i.e., knowledge of moral law). The responsibility of all people is to act as co-partners with God in eliminating evil from the universe.

IN SUMMATION

Kaplan's critics have concentrated on their attacks on his theology. To those who view the experience of God as unique or as an act of grace by a transcendent Being, Kaplan's theology seems much too impersonal. However, Jewish life, outside of Orthodox, has clearly been affected by Mordecai Kaplan. Among his many accomplishments are the following: his idea of Jewish community centers as social and cultural focal points for Jews to meet Jews; the equal participation of both Jewish men and women in ritual and the idea of *chavurot* as meeting places for study and the celebration of life-cycle events; and co-editing of *The Festival Prayerbook* (1958) and *The Daily Prayerbook* (1964). Most importantly, though, Kaplan founded the fourth denomination in Jewish life, Reconstructionism.

30

MILTON STEINBERG

BACKGROUND

Milton Steinberg was born in New York in 1903. He studied at City College in New York City and was ordained in 1928 at the Jewish Theological Seminary of America. While at the Seminary he identified with the teachings of Rabbi Mordecai Kaplan, founder of Reconstructionist Judaism. In 1933 he became the rabbi of the prestigious Park Avenue Synagogue and held that position until his death in 1950.

A student of Morris Raphael Cohen, Steinberg was concerned with a philosophic approach to Judaism, dealing with issues such as the nature of God, God's relation to man and history, the problem of evil, the confrontation of faith and reason, and the impact of non-Jewish thought on modern Jewish philosophy. His historical novel, *As a Driven Leaf*, used the Talmud as a background for defining theological problems. It deals with the heretic Elisha ben Avuyah and the conflict of religion and philosophy that his life represents. Elisha eventually realizes that both are based upon the acceptance on faith of undemonstrated basic premises. It is this realization that prevents Elisha from denouncing religion as inferior. His classic text entitled *Basic Judaism* sets down the fundamentals of Judaism.

Steinberg was also active in Zionist circles and devoted much time to furthering the Zionist cause in the United States.

GOD AND FAITH

Steinberg commences with the idea that it is impossible to ever know God completely, due to the limitations of the human mind. He therefore argues that one must accept God's existence on the basis of faith alone, for logic by itself cannot bring one to believe in God.

Steinberg posits a universe that is rational in the sense that all within it conforms to the law of its own being. This universe consists of living things which are purposeful. Because of this, Steinberg posits a Thought-Will as the essence of these things.

Regarding his views on God, Steinberg posits a God that is not only a Power but also a Mind. God is purposeful, ethical, and moral, a God who enters into relations with humankind. Yet, as a limited theist, Steinberg argues that God is not all-powerful. This conclusion is based on the fact that if humans are to have real freedom, God's control and power cannot be complete.

EVIL

Steinberg argues that nature is in the process of evolving according to God's will to higher levels. However, in every species of the universe there are found lower levels and stages of development. Evil, Steinberg posits, is to be found in these lower stages. In Steinberg's schematic of evil, God becomes exempted from the responsibility for the elements of chance occurrences of evil within the universe. Thus, for instance, if there is a tragedy, Steinberg would not say that it was brought about as a result of God but rather that it happened because of the lower levels of development within the universe.

Because certain aspects of nature are sources of evil, Steinberg advocates that humans have an important role in overcoming these limitations. God needs man's help in eradicating the evils of society. The challenge of evil requires a partnership between man and God to join hands in bringing light and goodness into the universe.

PRAYER

Steinberg asserts that prayer is the bridge between man and God. For Steinberg, any prayer or ceremonial is worship if it voices either the community or a single person speaking as a member of the group. To be efficacious, prayer must be sincere and genuine. Steinberg is critical of prayer that is rote and mechanical.

Steinberg also argues that prayer to be efficacious must be ethical, never seeking what is contrary to moral principle. Lastly, prayer to be efficacious must never seek the impossible. Thus, for example, one should not pray when one's wife is already pregnant that the child be a boy (or a girl). Such a prayer is nonsensical, for the sex of the child has already been predetermined prior to the recitation of the prayer.

JEWISH RELIGION

For Steinberg, the very word "Judaism" has two distinct meanings. Sometimes it denotes a full civilization, embracing both secular and sacred elements. Judaism also stands for something more limited: the spiritual aspect of that civilization; in sum, for the Jewish religion. It is in this latter sense that Steinberg uses Judaism in his book *Basic Judaism*.

Steinberg identifies the following seven strands that constitute Jewish religion:

1. A doctrine concerning God, the universe, and man

2. A morality for the individual and society

3. A regimen of rite, custom, and ceremony

4. A body of law

5. A sacred literature

6. Institutions through which the foregoing find expression

7. The people, Israel—the central strand out of which and about which the others are spun

Each of these seven strands is inextricably bound to one another, making Judaism into the living organism that it is. They are closely connected with one another, animated by a common spirit, and cannot, Steinberg maintains, be torn apart into separate strands.

IN SUMMATION

Steinberg's limited theism (similar to that of Rabbi Harold Kushner) is based on a God that is believed to be all-good, but self-limiting and not all-powerful. This explains the reason why evil pervades the world and undoubtedly offered a satisfying answer to those who questioned God's role in the evil that existed in the world.

Steinberg posited a challenge ahead, which included man and God joining forces in order to fight the source of evil and bring greater light into the world.

All of Steinberg's books enjoyed and continue to enjoy wide popularity among people who are in search of the basics of the Jewish religion. Several volumes of his essays were published posthumously: *A Believing Jew* (1951), *From the Sermons of Milton Steinberg* (1954), and *Anatomy of Faith* (1960).

31

MENACHEM MENDEL SCHNEERSOHN

BACKGROUND

Born in 1902 in the Russian-Ukraine town of Nikolaev, Schneersohn was early recognized as a prodigy in the field of Jewish studies. In 1929 he married Chaya Moussia Schneersohn, the daughter of the then Lubavitcher Rebbe, Rabbi Joseph Isaac Schneersohn, and went on to university studies in Berlin and Paris.

In 1941, escaping the Nazi occupation of France, Schneersohn emigrated to the United States, where he was put in charge of directing the social, educational, and publishing divisions of the Lubavitch movement.

In 1950 he ascended to leadership of the Lubavitch movement, the seventh leader to head the movement since its founding in the late 1700s.

The Lubavitch Hasidic movement was founded in Russia at the end of the eighteenth century. Today it is headquartered in the Crown Heights section of Brooklyn, New York. While most other Hasidic groups are insular, Rabbi Schneersohn has placed tremendous emphasis on outreach, particularly on influencing the nonobservant to accept Jewish ritual observances. The tactics used by Schneersohn's followers were very aggressive, including the sending of vans, known as Mitzvah Mobiles, into Jewish neighborhoods

Simply known as the "Rebbe" among his followers, his earliest extant manuscripts date from 1924, a collection of letters to Torah scholars containing responsa on Jewish legal and esoteric topics. Recently discovered journals of his writings reflect Schneersohn's creative interpretation of biblical, talmudic, and midrashic texts through the prism of Chabad Hasidism. To date, more than 200 volumes of his talks and correspondence have been published.

The following pages present gleanings from Rabbi Schneersohn's insights into a variety of social, moral, and spiritual issues that have confronted and continue to confront the Jewish people.

JEWISH UNITY

For Schneersohn, one of the comprehensive religious obligations of the Torah is the *mitzvah* of *ahavat yisrael*: love for fellow Jews, which is the basis of the entire Torah. Essentially, the *mitzvah* points to the unity of all Jews, as if they constitute a single entity. As such, any action by a Jew, whether negative or positive, is consequential to the entire Jewish people.

Schneersohn maintained that every Jew must remember that he or she is part of the whole Jewish people and representative of the entire Jewish people—the one people ever since the Torah was given at Mount Sinai, until the end of time.

The division of Judaism into branches such as Orthodox, Conservative, and Reform is artificial, for all Jews according to

Schneersohn have one and the same Torah, given by the one and the same God.

BODY AND SOUL

Schneersohn maintained that every human being is a composite of body and soul. Consequently, all his affairs and activities likewise contain elements of both body and soul—the material and the spiritual. One's routine activities are generally motivated by material and physical gain. Yet the soul within these routine affairs calls out for recognition, for the infusion of these ordinary affairs with an awareness of greater objectives and a higher purpose. Schneersohn held that the giving of charity and the support of Torah education for children are the spiritual incentives that ought to motivate a Jew in his or her daily activites.

Finally, the achievement of harmony between one's soul and one's material life is the achievement of harmony between the heaven and the earth.

THE HOLOCAUST

Schneersohn believed it unconscionable for anyone to suggest that the Holocaust was brought upon the Jews as punishment, for there is no conceivable sin that can call forth punishment of such great magnitude. Schneersohn therefore concedes that one cannot understand the Holocaust or ever presume to justify the horrific suffering of the people.

What one must learn from the Holocaust is the frightening consequences of a morality that defers to no authority higher than man, and the great depths to which even the most progressive civilization can fall when man is allowed to become the ultimate arbiter of moral judgment.

ISRAEL

Schneersohn maintained that God enabled the Jews to live as sovereigns in the Holy Land, a land promised to the Jews by God. This reality thus places a special burden and privilege upon the citizens of Israel and its government: to preserve the Jewish integrity of the country. Its educational system must be inspired by Jewish values and the tradition. In its relations with other nations, those responsible for representing its government in foreign affairs must assert its Jewish pride and traditions, which is certain to enhance the esteem with which Israel will be regarded.

EDUCATION

For Schneersohn, proper education is education whose purpose is cultivating a person's moral character. The development of a student's mathematical skills or knowledge of history and science cannot be divorced from his growth as a well-functioning member of society. Schneersohn advocates an educational program that rears children at a young age with a strong consciousness of a God who watches over them and bides them to conduct their lives with honesty, respect, and compassion for others. He further asserts that parents ought to serve as role models, with the school reinforcing the values.

SEPARATION OF CHURCH AND STATE

Schneersohn strongly advocates moments of silence for contemplation or prayer in public schools. He maintains that to deprive students of the freedom to affirm their faith in God in school is to give constitutional sanction to government interference with the people's religious expression.

He also maintains that the *menorah* represents the first triumph of freedom from religious suppression and advocates its presence on public grounds as a symbol of the great freedom upon which the founding fathers established America.

IN SUMMATION

Even after his death, the Lubavitcher Rebbe Menachem Schneersohn continues to command the largest Jewish army outside of Israel. His followers regard him as their commander in chief (some even regard him as the Messiah).

Because of his emphasis on outreach, there are today Lubavitcher representatives in hundreds of cities throughout the world.

The Lubavitcher movement also blazed a trail for the phenomenon known as the *baal teshuvah* movement. Many Jews have returned to their traditional roots as a result of contact with one of the many Chabad Lubavitch houses in communities and on college campuses.

The Jewish Day School movement, of which the Lubavitch movement was one of the earliest pioneers, has displaced the once prevalent ideology that Jewish education was only an appendage to the real business of acquiring a secular education.

32

JOSEPH B. SOLOVEITCHIK

BACKGROUND

Rabbi Joseph B. Soloveitchik, born in 1903 in Poland, is the preeminent figure of twentieth-century modern Orthodox Judaism. As Professor of Talmud at Yeshiva University in New York City, he ordained more than a thousand rabbis, probably more than any other person in modern Jewish history. Many of these occupy Orthodox pulpits today in the United States and Canada.

Until his early twenties, Soloveitchik devoted himself almost exclusively to the study of Talmud and Jewish law. He soon mastered his grandfather's method of Talmudic study, with its insistence on incisive acts, exact classification, and critical independence. At the age of 22 he entered the University of Berlin. There he majored in philosophy and was attracted to the neo-Kantian school. In 1931 he received his doctorate for his dissertation of Hermann Cohen's epistemology and metaphysics. In 1932 he emigrated to the United States, where he became rabbi of the Orthodox Jewish community of Boston. There he founded the first Jewish day school in New England, called the Maimonides School.

In 1941 Soloveitchik succeeded his father as professor of Talmud at the Rabbi Elchanan Theological Seminary of Yeshiva University. For many years he also lectured at the university's Bernard Revel Graduate School, where he served as professor of Jewish philosophy.

From 1952 Soloveitchik exerted a decisive influence on Orthodoxy in his capacity as chairman of the Halachah Commission of the Rabbinical Council of America (Union of Orthodox Rabbis). He also identified himself with the Religious Zionists of America (Mizrachi) and has served as its honorary president since 1946.

GENERAL PHILOSOPHY

Several intellectual approaches characterize the written papers of Soloveitchik. He retains more respect for human reason than does the unusual philosophic existentialist. Soloveitchik's main publication was a lengthy essay "Ish Hahalacha" in which his basic theological position was stated. On assessing the human situation, Soloveitchik maintains that man is viewed as both passive and active, object and subject. When a person lives in accordance with the *halachah*, that person becomes master of himself and the currents of his life. Such a person is able to control his thoughts, desires, and actions and stops being a mere creature of habit. His life becomes sanctified, and God and man are drawn into a community of existence that Soloveitchik termed a "covenantal community." This community brings God and man together in an intimate person-to-person relationship. For Soloveitchik, it is only through the observance of Jewish law that man attains the goal of nearness to God.

Soloveitchik stressed that in *halachah* nothing is holy and sacred until it is deemed so by man. Thus, for example, a Torah scroll is holy only when it has been sanctified by a scribe. He also pointed out that whereas Mount Sinai has not retained its holiness, Mount Moriah, where Abraham consecrated his ascent to God, became the site of the Temple and remained eternally holy.

THEOLOGY OF LONELINESS
AND THE SPLIT IN HUMAN NATURE

Soloveitchik's published papers center on the human condition and what it means to be a person in relation to God. Their main concern is to delineate the contradictions involved in being human and to illustrate how the *halachah* responds to our humanity. In specific theme—loneliness, anxiety, conflict—as in general outline, this is philosophic existentialism. Soloveitchik retains more respect for human reason than does the usual philosophic existentialist. He accepts science to the point of labeling as allegory the references in the blessing over the new moon to the ultimate perfection of its "blemish" (the Midrash says it was originally the same size as the sun). He does not believe that people whose lives are dominated by rationalism are unable to find God.

Much of Soloveitchik's writing is dialectical, in which he sees tension in every area of human existence. He makes no direct claim that everyone must see what he sees or that his is the only true understanding. He also maintains a fundamental dualism in human nature that is derived from the biblical creation stories. The Adam of one of these accounts is man the maker and controller, who strives to conquer the earth and use it for his good. He knows his limits and comes looking for God. The trouble is that he insists on understanding God in his own manipulative terms, a contradiction that he is unable to overcome and that sets up his conflict with the Adam of the second account of creation.

In this account Adam is the submissive servant of God. He is less concerned with creating his own world and accepts the world as God has created it. He sees God and hears God's command in every aspect of creation. In this very close relationship with God, Adam comes to know himself and recognizes his own uniqueness.

Since the first and second Adams are ideal types, Soloveitchik believes that people ultimately must live in both realms. Modern religion suffers because the first Adam is so dominant, culturally speaking, that only his manipulative way of thinking is acceptable. And anyone in whose soul the second Adam becomes foremost will feel an extra measure of loneliness in contemporary society.

HUMAN RELATIONSHIP TO GOD

Soloveitchik maintains a tripartite pattern when discussing the levels of human relationship to God. In level one, the most basic of all, people come to God in a vacillation of trust and dread, passive before nature and resigned to its laws. This level is a level of dependency. In level two, there is a relationship of love and fear of God. They are conscious of God's law and responsive to it, serving God out of an awareness that the law is God's gift to people, and observance of the law brings reward. In the third level, that of desire and clinging, every element of compulsion disappears, and people serve God out of complete freedom.

The highest form of relationship to God is when one lives according to the Torah and its commandments with great joy, always desiring to do the will of God.

IN SUMMATION

Soloveitchik is clearly the preeminent figure of twentieth-century modern Orthodox Judaism. In the many positions that he has held, he has become the spiritual mentor of the majority of the American-trained Orthodox rabbis. As chairman of the Halachah Commission of the Rabbinical Council of America, his halakhic decisions have been used by countless disciples and traditional Jews. Because the school that he headed, Yeshiva University, has always looked to achieve an integration between secular and religious studies, Soloveitchik has become a prime symbol of an Orthodox Judaism that attempts to achieve high levels of knowledge in both Jewish and secular studies.

33

Humanism and Eric Fromm

BACKGROUND

Eric Fromm, a social philosopher and author, was born in 1900 in Frankfurt, Germany. From 1929 to 1932 he worked at the Institute for Social Research in Frankfurt, but emigrated to the United States when Hitler came to power in Germany.

From 1941 to 1950 he served on the faculty of Bennington College in Vermont. He also served as professor at the National University of Mexico, Michigan State University, and New York University.

Fromm was a disciple of Ludwig Krause and Nehemiah Nobel and was greatly influenced by Hermann Cohen.

During his lifetime Fromm sought a rational solution to political problems. He was a pacifist and one of the organizers of the National Committee for a Sane Nuclear Policy.

Among his major concerns was how to deal with human isolation and doubt about the very meaning of life itself. He perceived that as a result of the rapid expansion of technology people were becoming more aloof and indifferent to the feelings of others. People need to have a sense of belonging and to associate with one another through personal intergrity and love. Fromm's recommendation of a return to a simpler life within the framework of a humanistic philosophy (i.e., asserting the dignity of man and his capacity for self-realization through reason) is described in such works as *Psychoanalysis and Religion, The Art of Loving,* and *You Shall Be As Gods.*

TWO TYPES OF RELIGION

Fromm believed that everyone has a religious need and that religion is "the formalized and elaborate answer to man's existence." He postulates two major kinds of religion: the authoritarian and the humanistic. Authoritarian religions emphasize the idea that human beings are controlled by a higher power outside of themselves. This higher power is "entitled" to obedience and worship. By submitting to the power authority of the deity, the individual escapes his loneliness. Fromm rejects authoritarian religions, for in them man is powerless.

On the other hand, humanistic religions (which Fromm does adopt) are centered around human strengths. In them, man experiences oneness with the All, achieving his greatest strength and self-realizaton, as in the Jewish prophets, where their doctrines have an underlying humanity and where freedom is the aim of life.

Fromm maintains that a person with a humanitarian conscience will never operate with the idea of pleasing or displeasing another. For a humanist, anything that furthers life is good, whereas anything that strangles it is evil.

Most religions, Judaism included, have gone through an authoritarian stage in which God appeared as a supreme Ruler and Commander. Fromm hoped that as religions develop, they will begin to recognize the many values of humanism.

GOD: THE HIGHEST VALUE

For Fromm, God is not a power that stands over people, telling them what to do or not to do in some celestial sphere. Rather, God stands for the highest value, the most desirable good. For Fromm, the most desirable good is the ability to develop one's powers to the highest potential. Thus for Fromm God is an ideal and a symbol in the minds of people, rather than a spiritual Being transcending humankind.

IMITATION OF GOD

If God is only a symbol for Fromm, then the question might be asked, "How does one get to know God?" Fromm maintains that at best it is only possible for man to establish a partial knowledge of God. Thus for Fromm, Judaism's essence is *not* knowledge of God, but rather, "imitation of God." This theological concept means that in order to better know God, one must act and practice in the same way that God acts.

The rabbis of old had already taught a similar concept. The Book of Deuteronomy states, "Follow the Lord your God" (13:5) and "walk in all of God's ways" (11:22). Is it possible for a person to follow God's presence? Rabbinic thinkers have explained that these verses are meant to teach that one should follow the attributes of God. The rabbinic authorities further define these verses by telling us that the instances recorded in the Torah of God's direct contact with the Patriarchs are designed to teach people how to act. One example of this is the following selection from Genesis Rabbah 8:13: "Just as God clothes the naked [Adam and Eve] so should we clothe the naked; just as God visits the sick [Abraham], so should we make it our duty to visit sick people."

Though people cannot become God in Judaism, they can be *like* God when they try to assume God's own attributes. Thus, life's goals for Fromm included speaking the truth, acting justly, and loving people.

IN SUMMATION

Fromm claimed that Judaism is an "untheological religion, where the stress is on the underlying substratum of human experience." He demonstrates using Judaic texts and in a nontheological way how the idea of God is a constant challenge to all kinds of idolatry.

Fromm urges that man move toward a humanistic approach to religion, emphasizing the necessity for people to develop their human qualities of love and reason.

Fromm is also a noted author. His works include *Man for Himself, Psychoanalysis and Religion, The Art of Loving,* and *You Shall Be As Gods*, a psychiatric commentary on the biblical view of God.

34

RADICAL AMAZEMENT AND ABRAHAM JOSHUA HESCHEL

BACKGROUND

Abraham Joshus Heschel, a European-born philosopher (1907), studied in Europe at the University of Berlin. In 1937 Martin Buber appointed him his successor at the central organization for Jewish adult education and the Juedisches Lehrhaus at Frankfurt on the Main. Deported by the Nazis in the fall of 1938, he taught for almost a year at the Warsaw Institute of Jewish studies.

He then emigrated to England where he established the Institute for Jewish Learning in London. In 1940 he arrived in the United States where he spent five years at Hebrew Union College in Cincinnati as associate professor of philosophy and rabbinics. From 1945 until his death he served as professor of Jewish ethics for the Conservative Movement's Jewish Theological Seminary of America.

Heschel was deeply attracted to Jewish spirituality in general, and to mysticism in particular. He wrote many books and studies on medieval Jewish philosophy, *kabbalah*, and Hasidism and became one of America's most influential modern philosophers of religion.

He was also a staunch religious activist, and in 1965 he marched arm-in-arm for civil rights with Martin Luther King, Jr.

In his later years Heschel was invited to teach courses on Judaism at the Union Theological Seminary of America, a Protestant Seminary directly across the street from the Jewish Theological Seminary. Since his death in 1972, Heschel has become one of the great heroes of the Conservative movement. Several Conservative day schools and honor societies have been named for him.

PHILOSOPHY OF RELIGION

Heschel sees the task of the religious philosopher as that of penetrating the reality underlying religion, the dynamic relationship between man and God, through the objective understanding of traditional documents of the Jewish people. Although he himself brings to the task the tools of modern philosophy, Heschel continues to point out that no amount of rational analysis can exhaust the fullness of this reality. Reason is limited in its attempts to disclose the Divine Presence.

Heschel's life works consist of two parallel strands: the study and interpretation of the classical sources of Judaism and the endeavor to offer an authentic theology that results from the application of insights from traditional Jewish sources to the problems that the modern Jew must face.

One of his earliest books, *The Prophets*, presents a phenomenology of prophetic consciousness. The first part of the book consists of an interpretive survey and commentary on the writings of particular prophets: Amos, Hosea, Isaiah, Micah, Jeremiah,

Habakkuk, and Second Isaiah. The remaining chapters deal with such themes as the prophetic view of history, justice and judgment, the divine-human relationship, as well as the diverse theories of prophetic inspiration.

In his Hebrew work *Torah min Hashamayim be-Aspaklaryah shel haDorot*, he presents the ideas underlying the Talmudic views of Torah and revelation. In his books *Man's Quest for God* and *The Sabbath*, Heschel addresses the topics of prayer and symbolism.

Heschel had always had a deep attachment to the State of Israel, and the crisis of the Six-Day War of 1967 challenged him to give theological expression to his views. In 1969 he wrote his book *Israel: An Echo of Eternity*, which dealt with his views and concerns related to the State of Israel. It contains a carefully reasoned apologia for the Jews' reclamation of their homeland, and a discussion of the significance of this event for Christian and Jewish theology.

Heschel died quietly in his home in 1972.

HESCHEL'S PHILOSOPHY

Heschel defines religion as the answer to man's ultimate questions. Since modern man is largely alienated from the reality that informs genuine religion, Heschel attempts to recover the important existential questions to which Judaism offers the answer.

For Heschel, God is a personal God who takes a passionate interest in His creatures. This so-called "divine concern" is the central category of Heschel's philosophy. The root of Jewish observance and ethics is, according to Heschel, man's ability to transcend his egocentric interests and to respond with devotion and love to the divine demands. The ability to rise to the holy dimension of the divine imperative is the ground of human freedom.

THE MEANING OF BEING HUMAN

Heschel's major work on the subject of the meaning of being human is entitled *Who is Man?* Heschel maintains that modern man must learn to understand himself as a uniquely centered self, a "who" rather than a "what"—a merely physical, biological entity.

For Heschel, true humanity begins with humility and reverence of life. The task of man is to become known to God, to listen to God, and to be judged by Him. It is on the basis of this line of thinking that Heschel declares, in one of his best-known aphorisms, "the Bible is not man's theology but God's anthropology."

Heschel maintained that the prophets taught that man's greatness is to be found in the fact that man is needed for something that transcends him. Happiness for Heschel is the certainty of being needed. And the Eternal God needs man for the effecting of his purposes in the world, and true fulfillment is to be found in the free acceptance of these purposes and the realignment of one's life so as to accord with them.

Heschel also speaks of man as God's ultimate concern. He suggests the following essential modes of being human: preciousness (dignity of human beings), uniqueness (no two individuals are ever exactly alike), opportunity (life is unpredictable, and man has a need for guidance from religious teaching), solitude and solidarity (being human implies the capacity both to stand apart and to share in community), reciprocity (know the meaning of both receiving and giving), and sanctity.

WAYS TO GOD

Heschel maintains that there are three routes to an awareness of God's presence. The first is the way of sensing the presence of God in the world, in things; the second is the way of sensing

God's presence in the Bible; and the third is the way of sensing God's presence in sacred deeds. These three ways correspond to the three great facets of religious existence as experienced by Judaism: worship, learning, and action.

For Heschel, one of the ways of becoming aware of God's presence is through worship and prayer. The predominant mood of Jewish prayer is that of praise. For Heschel, praise is the natural expression of what he calls "radical amazement," wonder, awe, and appreciation, which Heschel finds at the root of faith. The sense of wonder needs to be continually cultivated; thus, the need for continually repeated acts of worship and prayer.

Heschel distinguishes between two types of prayer: prayer as an "act of expression" and as an "act of empathy." In the former, the intention and the desire to pray come first, and the words follow. In the latter type, the words come first and the feeling follows. Both types of prayer are essential.

Heschel asserts that learning is the second great factor in Jewish existence, corresponding to Heschel's second way to God: the way of sensing God's presence in the Bible. Heschel holds that there is a hierarchy of moments within time. God is not equally available and communicative at all times. Therefore, one must learn to prize the specific moments of revelation and the record of such moments.

For Heschel, the Bible was given to the community of Israel. The mission of the Jewish people in Heschel's opinion is to be a community in which the Bible lives on.

The third way to God, in addition to worship and learning, that Heschel identifies is the way of action—the dimension of the deed. Heschel suggests in his writings that the venture of obedience to a concrete command (i.e., *mitzvah*) may in itself serve to quicken the sense of God's reality. Heschel believes that both the legal and nonlegal components of Talmudic literature are essential to a Jewish life of faith. To reduce Judaism only to law is to kill its essence.

Heschel uses the term "divine pathos" to characterize the openness of the Divine to human action. The Bible portrays a God who is a moral personality concerned with mankind, and especially Israel. Repeatedly, the image of the partnership of man and God is portrayed in the Bible in covenantal terms. When Israel acts as it should, God is made happy; when Israel transgresses, God is saddened and angry. Thus Heschel argues that God can be intimately affected by man's behavior, and that God possesses not only intelligence and will, but also feeling and pathos.

HESCHEL AND MEDIEVAL JEWISH PHILOSOPHY

Heschel was an acknowledged authority in the area of medieval Jewish philosophy. He wrote many studies on major figures of medieval Jewry, including Maimonides, Solomon ibn Gabirol, and Saadia Gaon. In interpreting their works, Heschel tried to portray them not as medieval rationalists but as deeply religious men whose philosophic works were primarily intended to show the limits of reason and validity of religious faith. In Heschel's work on Maimonides, he portrays Maimonides as a person who came to understand that godliness lies in prophet-like involvement with man rather than in and through removed philosophic enquiry.

Heschel's studies of medieval Jewish philosophy reveal a fundamental unity of outlook. In each there is a plea for existential commitment as the focus of authentic Jewish thought, a commitment that must translate itself into action.

IN SUMMATION

Of all the Jewish thinkers since World War II, Heschel has been one of the most productive and influential. His many writings have won him a wide following in the Jewish community as well as among Christian theologians.

Heschel was also a profound student and interpreter of Hasidism. His entire religious outlook was shaped by his Hasidic roots, and his vision of God's need for man is undoubtedly a product of Hasidic influence. In a number of studies of individual Hasidic masters who belonged to the immediate circle of the Baal Shem Tov, Heschel has provided one of the most profound images of the character of the Hasidic movement in its earliest phase.

Indeed Heschel's sound scholarship, philosophic vision, and ability to write poetically have given his work a unique authenticity and authority.

35

THEOLOGY AFTER THE HOLOCAUST

Jewish life and thought have been radically transformed by the Holocaust. The tragedy of the Holocaust and the incredible number of lost lives have left Jewish thinkers numb and many people with challenges to their faith in God.

The question of why there is evil in the world is as old in Judaism as the God-faith itself. Since no generation or individual has been spared the painful necessity of justifying God's way, the answers throughout the centuries have been quite varied. Following is a brief summary of the various answers in a search for an acceptable "theodicy" (i.e., an explanation of evil) that will reconcile the fact of it with the existence of God.

MORAL THEORIES

1. Evil is the result of some prior sin of the person on whom it was visited.

2. Evil may represent the expiation of the transgression of a community rather than the individual (i.e., individuals are held responsible for the sins of their community).

3. Evil is necessary for goodness and morality to exist.

4. Evil is indispensable to man's character since, were it not for its prodding, no one would ever bestir himself or develop attachments to justice and compassion.

METAPHYSICAL THEORIES

1. Evil has no reality itself but is merely the absence of good.

2. Evil only appears as evil because it is seen isolated or in a partial view.

EVIL IS TEMPORARY

1. Evil will be compensated and made good in the life after one's life.

2. Evil represents the survival into the human condition of other lower stages of reality out of which humans have emerged. The traces of evil are constantly being erased with time until the day when people will be perfectly human.

EVIL IS INSCRUTABLE

Evil is and always will remain a mystery, known only to God alone. This is the moral ending of the Book of Job, which states that it is not in our power to explain either the tranquility of the wicked or the sufferings of the upright.

Judaism has never promulgated one single authoritative "official" theodicy. It has always postulated choices and expects people always to recognize evil as something that needs to be combated.

THEODICY: THEOLOGIANS' RESPONSES TO EVIL IN THE WORLD

The focus of all theological speculation about the place of evil in the world is its relationship to God. The dilemma is: if God is all-powerful, then God is in some way responsible for evil. If God is not responsible, then God is not all-powerful. In that case, evil exists independently of God and God's sovereignty is then challenged. Thus the choice lies between these two options: an all-powerful God who is responsible for evil or a limited God who is not.

Chapters 36 through 39 present various modern theologians and their specific responses to the problems of evil, pain, and suffering in the world.

36

RICHARD RUBENSTEIN

BACKGROUND

Richard Rubenstein, rabbi and theologian, was born in New York City and ordained at the Conservative movement's Jewish Theological Seminary of America. After serving as rabbi in Brockton in the early 1950s, he became Hillel director at the University of Pittsburgh in 1958. In 1969 he was appointed adjunct professor of humanities at the University of Pittsburgh, and in 1971 he became professor of religion at Florida State University. He is a controversial theologian influenced by the "death of God" school in contemporary Christian theology.

"DEATH OF GOD" THEOLOGY

The theological problem raised by the Holocaust is the following: If God is the God of History and Israel is God's chosen people, what responsibility does God bear for Auschwitz? Did

God use the Nazis as the rod of His anger? The so-called "death of God" school movement developed in the 1960s as a Christian theological response to that era's sense of religious alienation, the constant presence of evil in society, and God's seeming indifference to it. Rubenstein's writings reflected his position that the horror of the Holocaust represented a radically new phenomenon that required a radical response.

The "death of God" phrase resonates with Christological overtones. Jesus had to die in order to accomplish his Divine mission, and his death allows for the vicarious atonement of human sins.

Rubenstein wrote *After Auschwitz*, a collection of essays dealing with the theological significance of the Holocaust. He maintained that God Himself did not die, but rather the human conception of God had died. The statement "God has died" means that after an experience as cruel and horrific as the Holocaust, one cannot any longer speak about a personal God who is all-powerful, loving, caring, and compassionate.

Had Rubenstein merely asserted the denial of God, his would not be a Jewish theology. What makes it Jewish are the implications he draws from his radical negation with respect to the people of Israel. It might be expected that denial of God's covenantal relation with Israel would entail the end of Judaism and its people. From the perspective of a traditional theology, this would surely be the case. Rubenstein, however, argues that with the "death of God," the existence of the community of Israel is all the more important. And the Jewish people need each other now more than ever.

Rubenstein replaces the traditional conception of God as caring and loving with a return to the mystical God who is totally undefinable and the source of all creation to which all creation ultimately returns.

Paradoxically, Rubenstein argues that in the age of the "death of God," people need religion with its rituals and traditions in order to deal with the many crises in their lives. The community of Israel is very important, and people need each other in order to create meaning in their lives. Judaism should continue as a means of helping individual Jews meet life's inevitable traumas.

Although Rubenstein's radical theology failed to strike deep roots into the less traditional Jewish theologians, his writings have given us a powerful image of what it means to draw the extreme conclusion that "God is dead."

PSYCHOANALYTIC INTERPRETATION OF JUDAISM

In many of Rubenstein's writings, he has carried on a reexamination of classical Jewish values for the modern, post-Holocaust Jew. Using psychoanalytic categories, Rubenstein has tried to reinterpret the meaning of classical aspects of Judaism while at the same time advocating their retention. Though these forms of religious life have lost their traditional justification, they still have, in his view, important psychological implications and thus need to be retained. In using the example of the Bar Mitzvah, Rubenstein sees this life-cycle event as a rite of passage, a ritual in which the community formally recognizes the sexual maturity of the boy, confirming upon him his masculine role as an adult member of the Jewish community. This is psychologically valuable for both the boy and for society. The synagogue thus retains its central role in Jewish life as a psychological clinic.

Rubenstein also maintains a desire for the modern Jew to recognize the priorities of nature. He posits that man must come to understand the real meaning of messianism as the proclamation of the end of history and the return to nature. The modern Jew must try to rediscover the sanctity of his natural life. Rubenstein thus sees the renewal of Zion and the rebuilding of the land with its return to the soil by the Jews as a forerunner of this return to nature on the part of the Jew who has been removed from the soil (symbolic of nature) by theology and necessity for almost two thousand years.

Finally, Rubenstein argues that anti-Semitism is a product of the mythic structures of Jewish and Christian theology. The contributing Jewish myth is its claim to be a chosen people, which has been disastrous for the Jewish people. The contributing Christian myth was predicted on its acceptance of the antecedent Jewish one: the Church accepted the chosenness of Israel and was therefore able to see it only in theological terms. In order to put an end to anti-Semitism, Rubenstein argues the necessity for the Jew to renounce his mythic self-image as a chosen people in order to normalize his relation with the Christians. Correspondingly, Christianity must demythologize its image of the Jew.

IN SUMMATION

A significant feature of Rubenstein's thought was his belief that with the demise of traditional Jewish theologies in the modern world, any transcendent meaning that could be attributed to Jewish destiny must of necessity be increasingly connected with the drama of the State of Israel. A politically avid supporter of Israel, he often attacked Jewish intellectuals of the "New Left" who impugned the Jewish state.

Rubenstein's volume *After Auschwitz* and his *The Religious Imagination* continue to be read by students of theology and philosophy as they reexamine classical Jewish values for the modern post-Holocaust Jew.

37

ELIEZER BERKOVITS

BACKGROUND

Berkovits, a rabbi and theologian, was born in Oradea Transylvania in 1900 and was ordained at the Hildesheimer Rabbinical Seminary in 1933. After serving in the rabbinate in Berlin, he left Germany in 1939 for England, where he served as rabbi in Leeds from 1940 to 1946. From there he served as rabbi in Sydney, Australia for five years. Then he emigrated to the United States where he served until 1958 as rabbi in Boston and subsequently as chairperson of the Jewish philosophy department of the Hebrew Theological College in Chicago.

As both a modern Orthodox theologian and a Zionist, Berkovits was much concerned with the tensions between a secular Jewish nationalism and Jewish religious tradition, a subject to which his volume *Towards a Historic Judaism* is devoted. In his work entitled *Faith after the Holocaust* (1973), he gives a traditional response to the Holocaust, pointing out salient elements that need to be considered in any response to Auschwitz.

RESPONSES TO SUFFERING

In *God's Presence in History*, Berkovits explores the various traditional historical responses to suffering in the Jewish tradition.

Berkovits explores Jewish tradition to see if anything can be taken from it that is applicable to one's response to the death camps. The first response and the most important in historical terms is that known as *Kiddush HaShem*: death for the sanctification of God's name. In traditional religious circles, martyrdom is viewed as the ultimate act of resignation and trust in God, both a testing and a response of faithfulness. During the Holocaust there were both those who were unable to face their end with faith and those who went to their death in joy that they could give their life for God.

Berkovits is critical of those who deal with the Holocaust in isolation, as if there had been nothing else in Jewish history but this Holocaust. He maintains that in the framework of Jewish history, Auschwitz is unique in the magnitude of its horror but not in the problem it presents to religious faith. Thus for Berkovits, the theological problem is the same whether one Jew or six million Jews are slaughtered. Each raises the same question, namely, How did God let it happen?

Berkovits rejects the response that the death camps are a result of the sins of the Jewish people. Acknowledging that the Holocaust was an "injustice absolute" that was countenanced by God, his concern is to make room for Auschwitz in the Divine scheme despite the fact that it is a moral outrage. It is here that Berkovits calls our attention to a sophisticated response to evil already stated in the Bible, the notion of *hester panim* (the hiding of God's face). *Hester panim* is the theological view that there are times when God will mysteriously, without any reason of human cause, hide from humanity. Moreover, Berkovits argues that God's hiddenness is a requirement for man to be a moral creature, for it creates the possibility for human action. By absenting Himself from human history, God allows humans freedom to be good or evil. Here Berkovits simply reasserts the classical view of the necessity of free will to morality. If God is strictly just, humanity would be impossible. Moral humanity requires freedom, and freedom will always be open to the possibility of abuse.

Berkovits maintains that God must also be present in order that meaninglessness does not gain final victory. Thus for Berkovits, God's presence in history must be sensed as hiddenness, and God's hiddenness must be understood as the sign of God's presence. God reveals His power in history by curbing His power so that man too might be powerful. The only enduring witness to God's ultimate power over history is the fate of the Jewish people and its history. In this history, Berkovits declares, we see both attributes of God. The continued existence of Israel despite its centuries of suffering is for Berkovits the greatest single proof that God is present in history despite His hiddenness.

ZIONISM

The last element in Berkovits' analysis of modern Jewish faith after the Holocaust is his fervent Zionism. He draws heavily on the theological implications of the rebirth of the State of Israel, stating that Israel's rebirth is contemporary revelation—the voice of God speaking forth from history. He further cites the events of the 1967 Six-Day War as having an especially revelatory quality to them. For Berkovits, the return to Zion is the ultimate vindication of God's presence in history. Whereas Auschwitz in Berkovits' philosophy is the hidden face of God, the rebirth of Israel is metaphorically the smiling face of God.

IN SUMMATION

Berkovits' more traditional response to the Holocaust continues to be taught and discussed in schools of Jewish philosophy throughout the world. Calling attention to a biblical response to evil in the Bible—the notion of *hester panim* ("hiding face of god"), Berkovits maintains that at times God mysteriously and without cause hides from man. God's hiding from man, Berkovits maintains, is required for man to be a moral creature. God's hiddenness creates the possibility of human action. This is a reiteration of the classical view that free will is necessary for morality to exist. With God's power limited, human moral action becomes all the more important if the world is to be redeemed. Like Fackenheim, Berkovits declares that the rebirth and continued existence of Israel despite its centuries of suffering is the greatest single proof that God is present in history despite His hiddenness.

38

IGNAZ MAYBAUM

BACKGROUND

A Reform rabbi and theologian, Maybaum was born in Vienna in 1897. He served as rabbi at Bergen, Frankfurt on the Oder and in Berlin. In 1939 he emigrated to England, and from 1947 through 1963 he was minister of the Edgeware Reform Synagogue in London and lecturer in theology and homiletics at the Leo Baeck College. Among his publications are *Sacrifice of Isaac* (1959), *Jewish Existence* (1960), and *The Face of God after Auschwitz* (1965).

RESPONSE TO JEWISH SUFFERING

For Maybaum, unlike Rubenstein or Fackenheim, Auschwitz is not a unique event in Jewish history, but a reappearance of a time-honored and holy event. A student of Franz Rosenzweig, Maybaum affirms the energetic relation between God and Israel, believing in the reality of the God of the Bible who established His covenant with the children of Israel.

For Maybaum, the pattern of Jewish history is one in which Israel's role is to be a nation among other nations and in which it is non-Jews who are the prime movers of events. From its inception in the Exodus–Sinai events, Israel's history is played out in relation to that of other people. It is for this reason that the categories of Jewish history have to be categories intelligible to non-Jews. Fackenheim introduced two categories to explain the structure of Jewish historic experience: "root experiences" (e.g., splitting of the Red Sea) and "epoch-making events" (e.g., destruction of the Jerusalem Temple). Maybaum, conscious of Israel's relations to non-Jews, subdivides Fackenheim's "epoch-making events" into two classes: *churban* and *gezerah*. *Churban* ("destruction") are events like the destruction of the Jerusalem Temple, which make an end to an old era and create a new one. *Gezerah* ("evil decree") are those events, such as the expulsion of the Jews from Spain which, although catastrophic, do not usher in a new era. According to this classification, Maybaum views the Holocaust as a *churban*, an event that signals the end of one era in Jewish history and the beginning of a new one. Whereas a *gezerah* can be averted (e.g., prayer, charity, and repentance avert the evil decree on the High Holy Days), a *churban* cannot be averted.

For Maybaum, there is a positive value in destruction. He cites the example of the destruction of the Jerusalem Temple as necessary for the creation of the Jewish Diaspora, which ultimately allowed the Jewish people to spread God's work throughout the world. The destruction of the Second Temple led to the establishment of the synagogue. Maybaum went on to posit that the Holocaust, the third *churban*, was the medium of spiritual development. It is framed in the shape of Auschwitz, an overwhelming reliving by the entire Jewish people of the crucifixion of one Jew, in order to be able to address the deepest sensitivities of modern Christian civilization. In Auschwitz Maybaum posits that Jews suffered vicarious atonement for the sins of humankind.

As a Reform Jew, Maybaum is able to interpret the destruction of Eastern European Jewry in the Holocaust as progress. Progress is understood by him as the freeing of the Jew from the *halachah* (Jewish law) and the enabling of political emancipation of the Jew and his enlightenment.

IN SUMMATION

Like Fackenheim, Maybaum is a man of faith, but more than Fackenheim, he is willing to draw the conclusion that other theologians will not draw: Hitler is God's agent, and God used him to purify and punish a sinful world. The six million Jews died an innocent death, having died for the sins of others. Furthermore, Maybaum wishes to emphasize that though one third of world Jewry perished in the death camps, two thirds survived. The miraculous survival of the two thirds is God's redemption, and thus Maybaum in his writings calls upon his fellow Jews to look at the redemption of the majority rather than dwell on the death of the sacred minority.

Maybaum was also an excellent preacher, and his sermons were published in several volumes. A jubilee volume was published on the occasion of his seventieth birthday.

39

EMIL FACKENHEIM

BACKGROUND

Born in 1916 in Halle Germany, Fackenheim was ordained at the Hochschule für die Wissenschaft des Judentums in Berlin in 1939. In 1940 he emigrated to Canada as an intern, serving five years as Rabbi at Temple Anshe Sholom in Hamilton, Ontario. In 1948 he joined the University of Toronto philosophy department and was made full professor in 1960. A religious existentialist, his works often grappled with questions of revelation as well as the problem of the evil in the world and the Nazi experience. Among his works are: *Paths to Jewish Belief* (1960), *Metaphysics and Historicity* (1961), and *God's Presence in History* (1970).

PHILOSOPHY

Few philosophers or theologians have written as extensively about the Holocaust as Emil Fackenheim. Himself a survivor of the camps, he has tried in his writings to grapple with the horrific events of the death camps in order to draw meaning from them for post-Holocaust Jewry. In his essays and in his volume *God's Presence in History*, Fackenheim has tried to find a way to avoid the perfect faith of the pious who see no special problem with the Holocaust and those like Rubenstein who argue the "death of God" theology and the absurdity of history.

Fackenheim maintains that to keep God and Israel together after the Holocaust is the demand of Jewish theology. Refusing to allow any theological explanation of the Holocaust to be given, he maintains that in no sense can any particular theodicy be offered in which God's goodness can be exonerated and Auschwitz seen as part of a rational cosmic pattern that humans can understand. In this sense, the Holocaust is devoid of explanation. Like Rubenstein, Fackenheim is unable to accept explanation that interpret the history of Auschwitz as occurring as a result of the sins of the people or martyrdom.

Despite the absolute failure of theodicy, Fackenheim calls on people to believe. He maintains that no one can understand what God was doing at Auschwitz or why He allowed it to happen. But, he posited, people must insist that God was there. Thus for Fackenheim, the Holocaust does not prove that God was dead, but rather that God addresses Israel.

Fackenheim maintained that revelation actually happened and that Israel's relation to the Divine is central. God is, for Fackenheim, continually present in history and, like Buber, he insists that God reveals Himself in history in personal encounters with Jews and Israel. Revelation is thus understood as the encounter of God and people, which happens everywhere and at all times.

JEWISH HISTORY: "ROOT EXPERIENCES" AND "EPOCH-MAKING EVENTS"

Fackenheim developed his own accounting of Jewish history, maintaining that Jewish history is a series of overwhelming events, but not all the events are of the same characters. The most powerful events, such as the exodus from Egypt and the giving of the Torah at Mount Sinai, actually created the religious identity of the Jewish people. These creative extraordinary events, all of which are public history happenings, Fackenheim calls "root experiences" that continue to claim the allegiance of the Jewish people. Thus, for example, the miraculous crossing of the Red Sea by the Israelites continues to be reenacted during the Passover Seder meal.

There is a second category of historical events whose function is different from that of the root experience event. Fackenheim calls these "epoch-making events," which are not formative and do not create the essentials of Jewish faith. On the contrary, they are historical experiences that challenge the so-called root experiences through new situations that test the adaptability of root experiences to answer to new historical realities. The destruction of the Jerusalem Temple, for example, tested whether the saving Presence of God could be maintained. The Talmudic sages and Jewish prophets were able to respond to these crisis situations, having faith in the root experiences of Israel and always believing that God would redeem the people of Israel in the future as He had in the past.

Indeed, the history of Israel in the Diaspora is a series of epoch-making events that continue to test Jewish faith and the God of History.

Fackenheim argues that the Holocaust is an epoch-making event in Jewish history that calls into question the historical presence of God. Yet, Fackenheim asserts, the Jew must still and always affirm the continued existence of God in Jewish history and must reaffirm the present reality of the people's root experience of a commanding God. Thus, for Fackenheim, the Jew must not reject God. Rather, Auschwitz itself is revelation in which Jews experience God as well.

Thus, for Fackenheim, Jews are under a sacred obligation to survive, always remembering the martyrs, and are forbidden to give Hitler posthumous victories. Paradoxically for Fackenheim, Hitler has made Judaism after Auschwitz a necessity. To say the "no" to Hitler is to say the "yes" to the commanding voice of the God of Sinai.

IN SUMMATION

Fackenheim adamantly refused to allow any theological explanation to be given of the Holocaust. Yet, despite this, he calls on people to believe and affirm the continued existence of God in Jewish history. Jews are under a sacred obligation to survive, and are therefore forbidden to despair of the God of Israel and God's redemptive powers. For Fackenheim, every Jew who has remained a Jew since 1945 has responded affirmatively to the commanding voice of Auschwitz. And the rebirth of the State of Israel in 1948 is living testimony to God's continued saving presence in history. According to Fackenheim, nothing else the Jews have done so fully sums up and projects the Jewish people's rejection of death and return to life.

40

Philosophies of Four Branches of Judaism: Orthodox, Reform, Conservative, and Reconstructionist

The institutions that the Jews around the world have built are impressive: thousands of synagogues, major rabbinic seminaries, Jewish community centers, religious day schools and yeshivot, Sunday and Hebrew schools, and many summer camps. All of these have been created in a little more than three centuries of Jewish life.

The American Jewish community of today is split into several major movements or branches of Judaism, just as its Christian neighbors are split into many churches. Sometimes these divisions have caused disharmony and disunity among the Jews, but they have also enriched Jewish life and thought by offering distinct choices in religious thought.

This chapter summarizes the religious philosophy of what are considered to be the four major branches of Judaism in America: Orthodox, Reform, Conservative, and Reconstructionist Judaism. Within each movement, of course, there are choices from within their religious-philosophic menu. American Orthodoxy is divided into many different groups and factions. Reform Judaism, believing in individual autonomy, allows considerable freedom of choice. Conservative Judaism and Reconstructionism also offer a variety of spokespersons on their behalf. The attempt in this chapter is to present the consensus of views of each movement's basic philosophy and principles. We shall begin with the earliest form of Judaism in America, namely, Orthodox Judaism.

ORTHODOX JUDAISM

Background

The oldest form of Judaism in America is Orthodox Judaism, often alternatively called Traditional Judaism. In fact, Orthodoxy was the only branch of religious Judaism in America until the 1800s when the Reform movement began to grow. The word "Orthodox" means "right belief" and was applied to Jews who refused to modify their observances and beliefs when they emigrated to the New World.

Orthodoxy was brought to America by the earliest settlers, most of whom were Sephardic Jews. By the end of the eighteenth and beginning of the nineteenth centuries, as more Ashkenazic Jews of German, Dutch, and Polish ancestry came to America, Ashkenazic customs began to replace the Sephardic ones.

Orthodoxy in America was not a new form of Judaism. It was a combination of the three types of European Orthodoxy: Spanish/Portuguese, west European, and east European. Among these groups there was basic agreement with regard to belief in a personal God, the binding nature of the Torah, the nature of *mitzvot* as God's religious obligations to people, and the *Shulchan Aruch* as the major code of Jewish law.

The great immigration of eastern European Jews to America brought with it a need for a good religious education. In 1886 the Etz Chayim Yeshiva was founded on the Lower East Side of New York to provide religious instruction for both students and teachers, as well as to hold worship services in accordance with Jewish law. In 1897 the Rabbi Isaac Elchanan Theological Seminary was organized on the Lower East Side to train older students. In 1915 the two schools merged with each other and became the nucleus of what today is Yeshiva University. Today it includes a full-scale program of both religious and secular studies and boasts of its own Rabbinical School which trains rabbis for the Orthodox rabbinate. Other Orthodox yeshivot and seminaries followed, and today there are hundreds throughout the United States and Canada. Many are administered by Torah Umesorah, the national agency for Orthodox, yeshivah education.

In 1898 the Union of Orthodox Jewish Congregations was established. Its purpose was to advance the interests of biblical, rabbinic, traditional, historical Judaism. The Union affirmed its belief that God had given the Torah and its laws and that the rabbinic interpretations in the Talmud and law codes were binding. The Union of Orthodox Jewish Congregations later added a women's division, a youth department called the National Conference of Synagogue Youth, and a college group known as Yavneh. The Union has also been active in supervision of the preparation of kosher foods throughout the country. Its symbol, the "U" encircled by an "O," can be seen on hundreds of food products throughout the country.

A number of synagogue groups in Orthodox life, including those of the ultra-Orthodox, have remained separate from the Union because they do not consider the Union to be sufficiently traditional.

One of the earliest Orthodox rabbinic organizations was founded in 1902, called the Agudat HaRabanim (Union of Orthodox Rabbis). As time passed, this union of rabbis was replaced by an American-trained Orthodox rabbinate established in 1935, called the Rabbinical Council of America. Today it is the largest and most representative body of the modern Orthodox rabbinate in America.

Basic Jewish Philosophy and Beliefs

God

Orthodoxy accepts the traditional views of God as developed in the Bible and Talmud and as taught in many of the medieval philosophic writings. To an Orthodox Jew, God is a spirit in the universe, creator of all that there is. God is omniscient, omnipresent, omnipotent, and eternal. God is aware of all that humans say and do. God's Will can best be understood by studying the Torah and performing its *mitzvot* (commandments).

Torah and Revelation

Central to the teachings of Judaism is the idea that God gave the Torah to His people. The Torah is the word of God, and just as God is eternal, so too is the Torah. This means that for an Orthodox Jew the Torah is not subject to change.

It is an Orthodox belief that the Torah is the revealed word of God, given at Mount Sinai. To be Orthodox, a Jew must be "Torah-true" and must believe that every word, law, and commandment of the Bible as interpreted by the rabbis is God's word and thus binding on every Jew. The rabbinic interpretations of the Bible always are true for all time, and thus must be observed by Jews in all ages. Accepting the divinity of the Torah in its entirety means that the Orthodox are not at liberty to make changes in its laws or reject any of its precepts.

The truly Orthodox Jew is characterized by his wholehearted observance of God's *mitzvot*, His religious obligations. An Orthodox Jew is prepared to make extensive sacrifices on their behalf and indeed shapes his entire life around them. According to the Orthodox, man's success in fulfilling his existential duty is to be measured in terms of how well he has ordered his life and his society in order to maximize fulfillment of God's commandments.

Although God revealed the content of the *mitzvot*, God did not always reveal their rationale. An Orthodox Jew is prepared to fulfill a *mitzvah* whether he or she understands its rationale or not. For an Orthodox Jew the *Shulchan Aruch*, the code of Jewish Law, is the most authoritative book of religious practices, spelling out in detail the commandments (both ritual and ethical) and how they are to be observed.

The highest priority of the Jew is the study of Torah, and immersing oneself in Torah study for the Orthodox is the most fundamental of *mitzvot* and the most sublime form of worship. As such, it must be a never-ending process pursued with equal enthusiasm and love by both young and old.

The Jewish People and the Land of Israel

Orthodox Jews believe in the biblical idea that the Jewish people are the chosen ones. Many understand this to mean that the Jewish people are commanded by God to be a holy nation, and that they were chosen to serve as a light unto the nations, living up to a higher standard of ethics and morality, of ritual and practice.

Orthodox Jews revere the land of Israel as the Holy Land. Most Orthodox Jews hope that the modern state of Israel will be operated according to the principles of the Torah and the *halachah* (Jewish law) will always set the guiding rules of the state. Rabbi Soloveitchik, one of the leading exponents of the Orthodox, always considered Israel to be a means to a higher end. In his view, Israel was to be the fulfillment of the destiny of the community of Torah people.

REFORM JUDAISM

Background

The roots of Reform Judaism (also called Liberal or Progressive Judaism) come from the beginning of the modern age in Germany.

Following the French Revolution, Jews in western Europe were afforded new freedoms. Those who tried to change Judaism to meet the needs of their new life gave birth to Reform Judaism. Several rabbinic conferences were convened between the years of 1844 and 1871 to try to work out the details and the shape that Reform Judaism would ultimately take. *Mitzvot* and customs, strict Sabbath and festival observance, and the use of only Hebrew for prayer were abandoned.

American Jewry too was eager for a Judaism that would be compatible with the times. Reform rabbis were imported from Germany, Bohemia, and Austria to lead many new congregations in places such as New York, Baltimore, Cincinnati, and Philadelphia. The Bohemian-born Rabbi Isaac Mayer Weiss came to the United States in 1846 and within fifty years helped shape Reform into a true and legitimate branch of American Judaism. In 1873 he established the Union of American Hebrew congregations, whose purpose it was to create a college for rabbis in the United States, to encourage the growth of new congregations, and to produce written materials for its religious schools. In 1875 Weiss opened the Hebrew Union College in his own synagogue in Cincinnati. After Weiss' death, an education department, a Sisterhood and Brotherhood, a School of sacred music to train cantors, and a youth department, called the National Federation of Temple Youth, were added. In 1889 the union of Reform rabbis, known as the Central Conference of American Rabbis, was founded.

In 1922 another great Reform leader, Rabbi Stephen S. Wise, established the Jewish Institute of Religion in New York. In 1948 it merged with the Hebrew Union College.

Today there are several Hebrew Union College campuses, including ones in Los Angeles and Jerusalem, Israel.

At a major convention in Pittsburgh in 1885, an eight-point program was adopted that was to set the tone for Reform Judaism for the next fifty years. The eight points were:

1. Judaism teaches the highest idea of God of any religion because it preaches ethical monotheism.

2. The Bible is the record of Israel's consecration to God.

3. Modern scientific and philosophic ideas are not opposed to Judaism since the teachings of the Bible merely reflect the primitive ideas of the time.

4. Only the moral laws of Judaism are binding. Ritual laws, such as kashrut and priestly purity, are no longer necessary to our spiritual upliftment.

5. We are no longer a nation, but a "religious community," and we no longer expect to return to Palestine or a Jewish state or offer sacrifices in a Temple.

6. Judaism must work with Christianity and Islam to bring truth and righteousness to mankind.

7. The notions of Heaven and Hell and bodily resurrection of the dead are no longer meaningful.

8. Jews must participate in the task of solving the problems of society through a program of social justice.

These eight points were so radical that they caused a split between the traditionalists and the liberals.

The year 1937 heralded the historic Columbus Platform, which marked the end of the older classical Reform movement, and the birth of a more traditionally oriented one. This Platform urged Jews to strengthen the Jewish people and rebuild the Land of Israel as a homeland, to develop synagogue and home rituals, to use home prayer and *mitzvot*, and to use the Hebrew language.

On the one hundredth anniversary of the founding of the Hebrew Union College, the Reform movement issued a new statement of principles called the Centenary Perspective. This platform affirmed the belief that the Jewish people is a unique people bound together by language, land, history and culture, and institutions, and inspired by its involvement with God. The platform also stated that Judaism emphasizes deed rather than creed as the most important expression of religious life.

Basic Jewish Philosophy and Beliefs

God

Reform Judaism is interested in theology. Adhering to traditional Jewish monotheism, it coined the term "ethical monotheism" to convey the belief that the world is ruled by one God whose primary demand is ethical behavior. Early reform rabbis described God as a spirit in the universe that maintains order in nature and morality in people. They did not accept the Orthodox view of a supernatural God who performs miracles such as the splitting of the Red Sea. For early Reform theologians, such biblical miracle stories are the tales about how people thought of God rather than how God actually operates in the world.

Modern Reform thinkers speak today of a more personal God whose spirit is present in the world and felt in history, especially Jewish history. Eugene Borowitz, a noted modern Reform theologian, asserts that the truest idea of God will inspire people to keep Torah in their lives and preserve the Jewish people.

Reform ideas about God are eclectic and diverse. Some Reform thinkers suggest that God is a part of nature and is the living power in the universe. Others believe that God is a force people feel as they struggle to evolve both physically and morally. The Centenary Perspective includes a number of statements about God, including the fact that affirmation of God has been essential to the Jewish people's will to survive. It further notes that throughout history God has been conceived and experienced in a variety of ways, and that humankind must continue to remain open to new experiences and conceptions of the Divine. Finally, the principles of the Centenary Perspective affirm that God is a reality and that human beings are created in God's image.

In summation, one could say that Reform Judaism commits its adherents to a sacred divine quest of searching for a God who may never be completely understood. But the quest itself will work to sanctify those in search with holiness.

Torah

Whereas Orthodoxy affirms that God revealed every word of the Torah to the Israelites at Mount Sinai and that every word is sacred and unchangeable, Reform philosophy generally affirms that only the ethical and moral Torah laws are eternally binding. Ritual laws and Sabbath restrictions were created by human beings for a specific time in history and therefore are not seen as divine and necessarily binding on Jews today.

Reform Judaism teaches that the Bible is the record of the religious experience of the Jewish people through many centuries of their life. Revelation, for Reform Jews, is a continuous process, and all truth is not limited to the Bible alone. Thus Reform Judaism believes that God did not reveal Himself only in a given period of history or only to a select group. Rather, it believes in the notion of progressive revelation, whereby God reveals Himself to people living in all generations. It also teaches that the Talmud and the huge body of rabbinic literature are human creations and neither eternally valid nor divine.

Mitzvot

Early Reform thinkers were negative toward the *mitzvot*, often writing that ritual commandments (e.g., Jewish dietary laws and dress) were old-fashioned and not in keeping with modern living and thinking. With the advent of Reform rabbis in the modern school, an increased emphasis on the need for concrete actions and symbols, *mitzvot*, and ceremonies was apparent. Today, the trend is one of an openness to return to *mitzvot* and more traditional practices and standards. Because of the notion of personal autonomy in Reform Judaism, the movement leaves it up to each individual to decide whether to follow a particular law. In addition, there has been in Reform Judaism a call for a guide to ritual practices within the movement. A number of such guides have been published, several of which call on Reform Jews to enrich their lives by observing *mitzvot* such as the lighting of Sabbath and festival candles, the abstaining from leavened food products on Passover, and the like.

The Jewish People

Early Reform thinkers announced that they were not a separate nation, but that their first loyalty was to the nation in which they lived. American Reform carried this idea even further by asserting that the Jews were no longer a nation but a religious community. Here the teaching was that the Jewish people no longer need to seek to return to the land of Israel because they already have a home. In the 1930s, however, a number of Reform rabbis and thinkers felt that Zionism was the hope of a Jewish future for many Jews, and the Columbus Platform of 1937 spoke of the "obligation of all Jewry" to aid in upbuilding Palestine as "the Jewish homeland." Today the modern Reform movement solidly supports the State of Israel and Zionism and has a presence in the State of Israel that includes a network of synagogues and a school of higher learning located in Jerusalem.

The Reform movement, unlike the Orthodox, rejected the idea that the Jews are the "chosen people" of God, substituting instead the "Mission" theory. This theory, introduced in 1885, teaches that Israel's Mission is to teach ethics, morality, and monotheism to all the peoples of the worlds. Israel must be, as the Prophet Isaiah urged, "a light unto the nations" in order to show the people the way of truth and justice. The Mission theory was changed slightly in the Columbus Platform of 1937, which referred to the Jewish people as a spiritual nation with a Mission— a responsibility to teach justice, spirituality, and morality.

Today the Reform movement's Commission on Social Action encourages its congregations to promote social action committees within the congregations. Reform Judaism is vitally concerned with issues of civil rights, religious liberty, hunger, and healing.

In Summation

Although classical and modern reform are different in their approaches on a number of issues, they share many ideas in common. Both see Judaism as a changing, evolving, and growing religion, a religion of the Jewish people. Both teach that the prophetic ideals of social justice and morality are the central ideas of Judaism. Both teach that *mitzvot* are not to be understood as God's law, but as the creation of human beings— creations that other human beings can change. And finally, both teach that Jews have a mission to spread monotheism to the world and to share moral and ethical ideals of the Jewish religion with all people.

CONSERVATIVE JUDAISM

Background

Conservative Judaism, like the Reform movement, had its beginnings in Germany. Those who thought that the Reform had moved too far in changing traditional practices sought a middle ground and organized a counter-Reform movement. The leader of this new Conservative group was Rabbi Zechariah Frankel of Prague, who in 1854 founded the Jewish Theological Seminary of Breslau. The group was given the name of the "Positive-Historical" school of Judaism, whose goal it was to preserve the *mitzvot* and Jewish law while at the same time to study the historical growth of Jewish laws and institutions in order to better understand Judaism.

The early builders of the Conservative movement in America were "traditional" Jews who disliked the extremism of Reform Judaism but realized the need to change and update certain Jewish laws and practices. At first some of them tried to work within the Reform movement but realized after the publication of the Pittsburgh Platform of 1885, which rejected ritual law, that a new rabbinic school and movement would have to be created. In 1886 Sabato Morais, rabbi of the Sephardi Mikve Israel Congregation in Philadelphia, founded a new Seminary called the Jewish Theological Seminary of America. Solomon Schechter became the school's first president, and at his insistence the school emphasized scholarship based on historical studies and criticism. During his long term of office, the seminary and the Conservative movement grew. A branch called the University of Judaism was opened in Los Angeles, the Jewish Museum was established in New York, and a school in Jerusalem was founded. In 1901 the Conservative movement's rabbinic organization, today known as the Rabbinical Assembly of America, was founded. Other organizations that have been added to the Conservative movement over the years include the lay organization of the movement, United Synagogue of Conservative Judaism, the National Women's League, the National Federation of Jewish Men's Clubs, and the United Synagogue Youth Organization. The movement saw one of its greatest periods of growth after World War II, as Jews moved from the cities into the suburbs. Finding few or no Orthodox synagogues there, and believing that Reform Judaism was too extreme, they chose Conservative Judaism.

In recent years, as the Jewish Theological Seminary of America was preparing to celebrate the one hundredth year since its founding, a joint commission was founded whose purpose it was to prepare an official statement of the philosophy of Conservative Judaism. The result of that commission was a volume entitled *Emet Ve-Emunah: Statement of Principles of Conservative Judaism*. Excerpts from this document will be used in the following summary of the principles of Conservative Judaism.

Basic Jewish Philosophy and Beliefs

God

Conservative Judaism believes in God but has taught varied views related to God. God permeates Jewish language, law, and lore. For some, belief in God means faith that a supreme, supernatural being exists that has the power to command and control the world through His will. For others, God's existence is not a fact that can be checked against evidence. Rather, God's presence is the starting point of one's entire view of the world and place in it. God is present when one looks for meaning in the world and when one works for morality and justice. In this view God is a presence and power that transcends humankind and that can be felt when we pray, study, and perform *mitzvot*.

God's elusive and mysterious nature has provided people with many options in deciding how to conceive of God.

Dr. Elliot Dorff identifies a list of common beliefs that Conservative rabbis hold regarding God. They include the following: there is a God, God is One, the world operates according to a moral order established and supervised by God, God takes an active role in human affairs, and man is God's partner in creation.

Revelation

Conservative Judaism affirms its belief in revelation, the uncovering of an external source of truth emanating from God. The exact nature of revelation has been understood in various ways by Conservative Jewish thinkers. Some believe that the revealing of the Torah happened only once in history, whereas others consider revelation to be an ongoing process by which each generation of Jews uncovers more and more of God's word.

Some conceive of revelation as the personal encounter between God and human beings. Among them are those who believe that during this personal encounter God communicated with people using actual words. For these thinkers, revelation's content is immediately normative, as defined by rabbinic interpretation. The commandments of the Torah themselves issue directly from God.

Others believe that revelation consist of an ineffable human encounter with God. The revelatory experience inspires the verbal formulation by human beings of norms and ideas. Still others conceive of revelation as the continuing discovery, through nature and history, of truths about God and the world. Proponents of this view tend to see revelation as an ongoing process rather than as a specific event.

Halachah: *Jewish Law*

Halachah consists of the norms taught by the Jewish tradition: how one is to live as a Jew. Most of these Jewish norms are embodied in biblical laws and their rabbinic interpretation throughout the centuries. Since each age requires new interpretations and applications of the norms, Jewish law is an ongoing process.

Conservative thinkers maintain that throughout Jewish history *halachah* has been subject to change. Most often new interpretation or application of existing precedents produced the needed development. Sometimes new ordinances were necessary.

For the Conservative movement (unlike in the Reform, where personal autonomy reigns supreme), each individual cannot be empowered to make changes in the law. Only the knowledgeable rabbinic community leaders are authorized by Jewish tradition to change and modify the law.

The Conservative movement asserts that the thrust of the Jewish tradition is to maintain the law and its practices of the past as much as possible. However, it further maintains that occasionally the integrity of the law must be maintained by adjusting it to conform to contemporary practice among observant Jews.

In order to make modifications or changes in *halachah*, the Conservative movement looks to its scholars of its various institutions. A Committee on Jewish Law and Standards has been organized to shape the practice of the Conservative community.

The Jewish People and God's Election of Israel

The Conservative movement places great stress on the concept of Jewish peoplehood. It preaches the importance of *klal yisrael*, the world Jewish community, and the responsibility of all Jews to help one another.

The Conservative movement also accepts the idea of the chosen people. Israel was chosen by God for a special purpose or reason: to spread the teachings of the Torah to the nations of the world. But being chosen is not so much a privilege as a duty, for Jews are expected to live up to a higher standard of ethics and behavior.

The State of Israel and the Role of Religion

The Conservative movement has always been in favor of the reestablishment of the State of Israel. It asserts that Israel ought to be a democratic state that safeguards freedom of thought and action of all its citizens. On the other hand, it posits that Israel ought to be a distinctively Jewish state fostering Jewish religious and cultural values.

The Conservative movement further posits that the laws

passed by the State of Israel should never be used to support a single religious view or establishment to the exclusion of others. It thus favors religious pluralism and is currently lobbying for the State to permit all rabbis, regardless of affiliation, to be able to perform religious functions.

Finally, the Conservative movement encourages and cherishes *aliyah* to Israel as a value, goal, and a *mitzvah*. It promotes both adult and teen visits to Israel throughout the year.

Social Justice

The Conservative movement has an honorable history of concern for social justice of Jews and non-Jews alike. Over the years the various arms of the movement have issued significant statements on the need to deal with the many social injustices of our times. Today its Committee on Social Action has worked to establish programs to help eliminate poverty and homelessness as well as to aid, feed, and shelter the hungry.

The Ideal Conservative Jew

Three characteristics are identified in the *Statement of Principles of Conservative Judaism* that mark the ideal Conservative Jew:

1. First, he or she is a willing Jew, committed to observing *mitzvot* and to advancing Jewish concerns. This would include both deeds of social justice as well as observance of the Jewish dietary laws, the Sabbath, and holidays.

2. He or she is a learning Jew, able to read Hebrew and acquainted with contemporary Jewish thought and other Jewish classics. Learning is a lifelong quest through which Jewish and general knowledge must be integrated.

3. He or she is a striving Jew. No matter the level at which one starts or the heights of piety and knowledge one attains, what

is needed is an openness to those observances one has yet to perform and the desire to grapple with critical issues one has yet to confront.

RECONSTRUCTIONIST JUDAISM

Background

The youngest of the religious movements in American Judaism is the Reconstructionist movement. Unlike the three other branches of Judaism, it is particularly an American movement. The movement is based on the work of Rabbi Mordecai Kaplan, who in 1940 founded the Reconstructionist foundation. In 1959 Rabbi Ira Eisenstein, Kaplan's son-in-law and close associate, formed the Fellowship of Reconstructionist Congregations. Today the movement is known as the Federation of Reconstructionist Congregations. In 1968 the Reconstructionist College to ordain rabbis was founded in Philadelphia, and in 1974 the Reconstructionist Rabbinical Association was created, the Union of Reconstructionist rabbis. Today Reconstructionist Judaism is the fourth major movement in Jewish life.

The essence of Kaplan's Reconstructionist approach is a reconstruction of Jewish ideas, life, and philosophy. The seal of the Reconstructionist movement explains its goals. Its form is that of a wheel. The hub of the wheel is Israel, the center of Jewish civilization from which all other Judaic forces radiate. Religion, culture, and ethics are the spokes of the wheel by which the influence of Israel is felt on Jewish life everywhere. The wheel has both an inner and an outer rim. The inner rim represents the Jewish community tied to Israel, even though it is spread throughout the world. It is attached to Israel by bonds of religion, ethics, and culture. The outer rim is the general community, in which the Jewish civilization maintains contact at every point. The seal thus symbolizes the philosophy of Reconstructionist Judaism.

Basic Jewish Philosophy and Beliefs

God

Mordecai Kaplan's ideas about God are anything but traditional. Philosophically speaking, he is considered both a humanist and a naturalist. He is a humanist because he finds God in people and in human experience. Kaplan also finds evidence of God in nature, because the world has order, laws, and design.

Kaplan defines God as the power or process that makes for salvation and fulfillment. He believed that people have in them a force or power driving them to reach for ideals such as justice and truth and peace. That power is what he calls God.

The radical change in the way Kaplan thinks about God is his idea that God's power is limited. Reconstructionists believe that there are things that are within God's power and things that God cannot control. That part of life and the world not yet filled with God's presence is the evil part of life.

Torah

Reconstructionism does not believe that God revealed the Torah to Moses at Sinai. The Reconstructionists accept the thinking of modern biblical scholars who basically assert that the Bible is the work of many people over a period of time. Mordecai Kaplan wrote that the Bible is not the record of God's work to human beings, but of peoples' search for God. Whenever one discovers a truth or moral idea, that is the revelation of God's will.

Because of this view, Reconstructionists do not believe that *halachah* is holy and unchangeable and do not speak in terms of *mitzvot*. Instead, Reconstructionists generally call the *mitzvot* "folkways" and "customs." Every people in history has created its own folkways and customs. Jewish folkways and customs are intended to bring people closer to God and to help them lead more meaningful lives.

Kaplan always taught that the people, not the rabbis, must have the final say in whether to accept or drop a custom. In Kaplan's own congregation, the Society for the Advancement of Judaism, the entire membership voted for or against ritual changes, thus making the congregation one of the most democratic of all.

The Jewish People

Reconstructionism places a heavy emphasis on the Jewish people, the center of Jewish civilization. For Reconstructionists, the purpose of the civilization is to keep the Jewish people alive and vibrant and to create values that add worth to human life. Kaplan did not call the Jewish people a "chosen people." In place of the idea of chosenness he taught the idea of "Mission," and he advocated a Jewish existence whose purpose it was to foster both within Jews themselves as well as the world at large a sense of moral responsibility in action.

The Land of Israel

By and large, Reconstructionists believe that a full Jewish life is possible only in the Land of Israel. However, Kaplan rejected the Zionistic imperative that all Jews must emigrate to Israel, knowing full well that this was unrealistic. He also very much opposed the Orthodox view that Israel must be a Torah state, run according to Jewish law without separation of religion and government.

Kaplan advocated that Israel become a cultural and spiritual center that would guide world Jewry. A creative partnership between Israel and Jews around the world would help to revive the spirit of the Jewish people.

Social Action

Kaplan and the Reconstructionists have taught that the goal of religion is to bring salvation to the group and not just to the individual. This could only be achieved if the religious principles and beliefs were translated into moral action. From its inception, the Reconstructionist movement has been involved in a plethora of social action issues.

In Summation

Mordecai Kaplan saw Judaism in America not as a singular irrelevant element in a vast secular landscape, but as an evolving civilization that would grow to touch every aspect of an American Jew's life. He defined that civilization as consisting of peoplehood (a shared history and destiny), an attachment to the State of Israel and to the Hebrew language, a sense of uniqueness and of Jewish destiny growing out of the study of Jewish literature, and a belief that Jewish history and literature have provided invaluable wisdom by which to live. The revolution in Kaplan's Reconstructionist thinking was that he conceived of Judaism as a civilization and rejected the concept of chosenness. This did not mean that he advocated dispensing with theology or ritual. Religion, he insisted, was the historic and unique way by which Jewish people can remember collectively the great moments in their history and together rededicate themselves to spiritual values that transcend any one individual person or society in time. But religion was only a part, as Kaplan saw it, of a total civilization that needed to evolve into a new and modern form.

GLOSSARY OF PHILOSOPHIC TERMS

The glossary is intended to present brief and concise explanations of the basic, the sublimely sophisticated, and even the most complicated beliefs of Jewish philosophy as well as a cross-section of biographical sketches of those philosophers who have contributed to the rich philosophic culture of Judaism.

Abraham ben Moses ben Maimon (1186–1237): The only son of Maimonides, he believed that one's destiny is completely within the hands of God and that the realization of human ideals depends at every moment on the will of God. He accepted the importance of reason, but was greatly removed from his father's rationalism.

Abravanel, Isaac (1437–1509): The last of the great Jewish Spanish statesmen whose encyclopedic knowledge included Christian literature. Although he wrote a commentary on the *Guide for the Perplexed*, he moved toward dogmatism. He also argued that Judaism cannot be reduced to a creed since every verse in the Torah is to be given unconditional credence.

Abravanel, Judah (ca. 1460–1523): Known among Christians as Leone Ebreo, he was the son of Isaac Abravanel. His philosophy gave emphasis to the esthetic direction of the Platonic form of thought, with God the source of all beauty. His central doctrine is that love streams from God to His creatures and creations.

Abulafia, Rabbi Meir ben Todras (ca. 1170–1244): One of the most renowned rabbis of Spanish Jewry in the first half of the thirteenth century, his work focused on Jewish law, Maimonides' interpretation of resurrection, and Hebrew poetry.

After Auschwitz: A book by Richard Rubenstein that focuses on the controversies that developed in the 1960s regarding the existence of God in the light of the evil of the Holocaust. Its influence shaped the form these controversies took and became the fabric for the philosophic consideration of God in the modern era tainted by the death of six million Jews.

Agnosticism: Refers to a neutralist view on the question of the existence of God.

Ahad Ha'Am (1856–1927): The pen name of Asher Ginzberg. He thought that science had refuted religion and substituted a high level of appreciation for humanity and the notion of nationhood for God and revelation. He was considered the foremost proponent of cultural or spiritual Zionism, believing that the Jewish people had a genius for high culture that was centered on ethics and that the revised state was to be the spiritual center of Judaism.

Albag, Isaac: Thirteenth-century philosopher of southern France and northern Spain, he was one of the first philosophers to maintain the doctrine of the double truth. He claimed that philosophic knowledge does not have to conform to the teaching of revelation. Contradictions may be answered from the perspective of facts and not from the perspective of philosophy without harming either knowledge or revelation.

Albo, Joseph: Fifteenth-century philosopher and student of Hasdai Crescas. He is best known for his *Book of Principles*, which was devoted to a discussion of dogma. Albo's basic principles of Judaism were revelation, God, and reward and punishment.

Anan ben David: Eighth-century ascetic sage in Babylonia, considered by the Karaite sect to be their founder.

Anthropomorphism: Ascription of human form and characteristics to God.

Aristobolus of Paneas: Jewish Hellenistic philosopher who lived in the first half of the second century B.C.E. He utilized allegory to interpret the Bible.

Articles of Faith, Thirteen: Articulated by Maimonides as the minimum of Jewish philosophic knowledge in his Commentary on the Mishnah. These truths include the existence of God, God's unity, God's incorporeality, God's eternity, the obligation to worship one God, there is prophecy, Moses is the greatest prophet, the Torah is of divine origin, the eternal validity of the Torah, God knows the deeds of human beings, God metes out reward and punishment, God will send a messianic redeemer, and God will resurrect the dead.

Atheism: The disbelief in the existence of a deity.

Azriel of Gerona (thirteenth century): One of the earliest and most profound thinkers of kabbalistic mysticism.

Baal Shem Tov: Literally "master of the good name," this name was given to the founder of hasidism, Israel ben Eliezer (1700–1760), a charismatic figure who became known through the oral tradition of his students who handed down his stories and tales.

Bachya ben Joseph ibn Pakuda: A moral philosopher who lived in Spain in the latter half of the eleventh century. His best-known work was *Duties of the Heart*, which focused on the obligation of the individual regarding his inner life, rather than his actions.

Baeck, Leo (1873–1956): A liberal theologian, he had a unique nonphilosophic approach to human piety and believed that ethics without religious certainty is reduced to mere moralism. He also contended that evil was the misuse of human freedom.

Berkovits, Eliezer (1900–): Orthodox rabbi whose contribution lies in his understanding of the Holocaust. He maintained that those who were not in Nazi death camps do not have the right to say whether God was there or not. He contends that those who believe that God was not in the concentration camps extrapolated from the few disillusioned survivors who denied God's presence. Instead, Berkovits gains strength of faith from those who were there and whose belief in God grew stronger as a result.

Bernays, Isaac (1792–1849): Chief rabbi of Hamburg whose name is associated with the *Biblical Orient*. This volume attempts to interpret the historical development of the spirit in a philosophic way.

Binah: Insight and understanding; the third *sefirah* in the kabbalistic understanding of the world.

Borowitz, Eugene B. (1924–): Reform rabbi and leading liberal theologian whose work focuses on an exploration of autonomy in decision-making and a covenant theology in explaining the relationship between God and the individual.

Breaking of the Vessels: According to Isaac Luria, at creation the vessels holding the upper three *sefirot* kept the divine light that flowed into them. The light that struck the next six, however, was too strong and broke and scattered the vessels and the light that they held.

Buber, Martin (1878–1965): A religious existentialist influenced by hasidism, most remembered for his dialogic I and Thou approach to the relationships with God and between people.

Catholic Israel: Term coined by Solomon Schechter to refer to the entire community of Israel, synonymous to *"klal yisrael."*

Chafetz Chayim: Literally meaning "desirous of life." Rabbi Israel Meir haKohen wrote a book by this title dealing with ethics. He himself is also referred to as "the Chafetz Chayim."

Chochma: Wisdom, also the second level of the kabbalah notion of *sefirot.*

Chosen People: Often referred to as the election of Israel, it refers to the selection of the Jewish people by God for the revelation of the Torah.

Cohen, Hermann (1842–1918): Philosopher whose work best exemplified a synthesis of Jewish philosophy and German idealism that grew out of his concern for ethics.

Commandments of Obedience: A notion of Saadia Gaon that distinguishes between rational commandments that revelation reiterates and the commandments of obedience that are exclusive to revelation and include the cultic and ceremonial laws of the Bible.

Conservative Judaism: The organized, institutionalized system of Judaism that follows the Historical School. It maintains a traditional view on law, which holds that contemporary decisions should be fixed by a body of rabbinic experts and interpreted by local rabbis. Its watchwords are "tradition and change."

Cosmogony: Theory of the origin of the universe.

Cosmology: Metaphysics that deals with the universe as an orderly system.

Costa, Uriel da (1585–1640): Philosopher born into a Marrano family in Portugal. After his book *Examen dos Tradicoens Phariseas Conferidas* was burned, he criticized the rabbinic community for being too ritualistic. In particular, he believed that the doctrine of immortality of the soul was questionable and not derived from the Bible.

Covenant Theology: A theological system based on the fundamental relationship in which the individual Jew stands, namely the covenant. This covenant was made and also maintained in the context of the community where the individual Jew's relationship with God was established.

Creatio ex Nihilo: Creation from nothing; the theological notion that God created the world out of nothing.

Cresdas, Hasdai (ca. 1340–1410): One of the most influential leaders of Spanish Jewry, his magnum opus was entitled *Or Adonai* (*Light of the Lord*), a collection of dogmas.

"Death of God": Philosophic and theological post-Holocaust concept that God "died" because God did not stop the events of the Holocaust.

Devekut: Literally, the cleaving of a person to God. A mystical concept.

Divine Attributes: Characteristics or behaviors of God.

Dogmas: Statements related to essential principles of belief. Examples in the Jewish world include Joseph Albo's *Ikkarim* (*Basic Principles*) and Maimonides' *Thirteen Articles of Faith*.

Eclipse of God: Like the Hebrew *hester panim*, this is when God hides His face, often as a form of retribution.

Emunah: Faith, one of the levels of the *sefirot*, according to kabbalah.

Enlightenment: Also called the Haskalah. In Eastern Europe it refers to the middle of the eighteenth century and beyond when, for the first time, the major streams of European thought came into contact with and influenced the world of Judaism, both socially and spiritually. This contact had a significant impact on Jewish philosophy. One of the first representatives of this type of philosophy was Moses Mendelssohn.

Epikoros: Also spelled *apikoros*, a rabbinic term for a nonbeliever or a skeptic.

Essence of Judaism, The: Leo Baeck's first book in which he maintains that ethical monotheism is the essence of Judaism.

Eternal Thou: In Martin Buber's view of the world, the potential relationship one has with God is the model for all relationships. In this way God is called the Eternal Thou.

Ethical Monotheism: The notion that this is the essential element of Judaism once all ritual and ceremony is stripped away. The belief in one God who is the standard for ethics in the world.

Everything is foreseen, yet permission is given: The

classic statement of Rabbi Akiba in *Ethics of the Fathers*, which expresses the reconciliation between God's omniscience and the notion of free will. The individual is free to do what is chosen, but God knows ahead of time what the choice will be.

Everything is in the Hands of Heaven: The classic philosophic statement that expresses utter abandon to God, who is in control of everything in the world.

Existentialism: Movement in philosophy that stresses that people are entirely free and therefore responsible for what they make of themselves.

Fackenheim, Emil (1916–): Reform Jewish theologian and philosopher, most significant for his discussion of themes of the Holocaust. He maintained that God was absent in the Holocaust, arguing that the Holocaust marked a new level of human evil, and the Jewish response to it is a new revelation—the absolute commitment of the Jewish people is a response to the absolute end of the Nazis.

Feinstein, Moshe (1895–1989): Twentieth-century Orthodox rabbi, head of Metivta Tiferet Jerusalem in New York, Feinstein became the leading Halakhic authority of his time.

Formstecher, Solomon (1808–1889): Author of *Die Religion des Geistes* (*Religion of the Spirit*), an attempt to provide a philosophic basis of Judaism. His concept of religion flows from metaphysical presuppositions borrowed from Schelling. His philosophic approach to ritual and ceremony laid the foundation for the Reform branch of Judaism.

Frankel, Zechariah (1801–1875): Rabbi and scholar, he became chief rabbi at Dresden in 1836. From 1854 until his death he directed the Breslau Rabbinical Seminary, which endeavored to combine Jewish religious tradition with the European Enlightenment.

Free Will, Doctrine of: Philosophic notion that allows for the individual to select a course of action from a number of choices and is the cause of the action that results from his choice.

Gabirol, Solomon ibn (ca. 1020–1057): Poet and Spanish

philosopher, his writings reflect mystical tendencies and scientific knowledge. His major philosophic work is called *Mekor Chayim*, devoted to the issues of matter and form.

Geiger, Abraham (1810–1874): Early leader of Reform Judaism, he was active in the synods held by Reform rabbis in Frankfurt and Breslau and a founder of the Breslau Seminary.

Gershom, Levi ben (1288-1344): Also known as Gersonides, or the RaLBaG, he was a philosophic commentator on the Bible. As a commentator, he extracted the ethical, religious, and philosophic teachings from the text.

Gnosticism: Reflecting a schism in the world between light (good) and darkness (evil), it is a mystical system, based on gnosis (knowledge of God).

Guide for the Perplexed: The major work of Maimonides in which he reveals the hidden philosophic truths inherent in the Bible.

Halevi, Judah (1085–1141): Poet and philosopher who settled in southern Spain. He belonged to no one philosophic school, considering philosophy arbitrary. One of his best known works is *The Kuzari*.

Hasidism: A traditional religious movement, devoted to strict observance of Jewish ritual, founded by the Baal Shem Tov in the eighteenth century. It is dominated by a communal structure that focuses on ecstasy and mass enthusiasm.

Heschel, Abraham Joshua (1907–1972): Philosopher who attempted to illumine the relationship between God and people. He argued that religion has faded in the modern world because we have not attempted to recover the dimension of reality in which a divine encounter might take place.

Hester Panim: Referring to God when He hides His face as a sign of retribution.

Hirsch, Samson Raphael (1808–1888): Likely the foremost spokesperson for Orthodox Judaism in the nineteenth century in Germany. He is best known for the focus of his philosophy, quoted from the Ethics of the Fathers 2:2, "The study of the

Torah is excellent together with *derech eretz* (worldly occupation)."

Historical School: The basic approach of Conservative Judaism, and synonym for the movement in Europe, it was an alternative religious response to emancipation and the position Jews found themselves in as a result.

Hochschule für die Wissenschaft des Judenthums: Center for the Scientific Study of Judaism. Liberal rabbinic seminary in Berlin, established in 1872 until 1942.

Humanism: Antithetical to supernaturalism, humanism regards God as man's highest aspirations, reflecting man's pursuit of ideal values and embodying the sum of humanity.

I and Thou: The phrase associated with the philosopher Martin Buber that epitomizes a belief that all experience is based on relationships. Everyday experiences are "I–It," but real communication between people is on a higher level (reflected by a relationship between the individual and God, the Eternal Thou).

Judaism as a Civilization: The magnum opus of Mordecai Kaplan, in which he articulates the philosophy of Reconstructionism and the foundational principle that Judaism is more than a religion. Rather, it is a civilization that encompasses religion, language, history, and spiritual and ethical ideals.

Kalam: Arabic scholastic theology that influenced, in particular, the Jewish philosophers of the Middle Ages, notably Saadia Gaon.

Kaplan, Mordecai (1881–1983): Philosopher and founder of Reconstructionism. He defined Judaism as an evolving religious civilization. He also developed the idea of Bat Mitzvah and the concept of a synagogue center.

Karaism: A sect founded by Anan ben David that developed in the eighth century and relates solely to the written biblical tradition as opposed to the Oral Law.

Kelippot: Literally "shells," referring kabbalistically to the forces of evil that dominate the spiritual lights originally emanating from creation.

Klatzkin, Jacob (1882–1948): Author, philosopher, and Zionist. He was a student of Hermann Cohen, whose philosophy focused on culture and art.

Krochmal, Nachman (1785–1840): Referred to as the ReNaK, Krochmal was a philosopher and historian who is considered one of the founders of the Wissenschaft des Judenthums. His philosophy of history is based on an assumption that history depends on spiritual content.

Kushner, Harold. Twentieth-century Conservative rabbi who wrote of a limited God in the 1981 best-selling volume *When Bad Things Happen to Good People.*

Kuzari, The: Written by Judah Halevi in an attempt to answer questions posed by a particular Karaite, it is a work against Aristotelianism, as well as Christianity and Islam.

Levinas, Emanuel (1905–): French philosopher who focuses on the significance of the other in metaphysics.

Liberal Judaism: A general term for nontraditional Judaism that often includes Conservative, Reform, and Reconstructionism. It is probably most often used today as a synonym for Reform Judaism.

Liebman, Joshua Loth (1907–1948): Reform rabbi who gained a national reputation after publishing *Peace of Mind*, a pastoral volume, offering solace to an America that had suffered during World War II.

Logotherapy: A term coined by Victor Frankl from the Greek word *logos* or the human spirit. A meaning-centered psychotherapy based on a philosophy that focuses on man's orientation to meaning. Frankl believed that the human spirit is the treasure chest for the most unique human resources.

Lubavitch Hasidism: Lubavitch was a small town in Russia that became the center of Chabad, when the son of the founder moved the hasidim from Lyady in 1813. Today the Lubavitch hasidism can be found in cities and towns around the world. Its most recent leader was Rabbi Menachem Mendel Schneersohn.

Luria, Isaac Solomon (1534–1572): Called Ha-Ari (sacred lion), he was a kabbalist whose unique brand of mysticism became known as Lurianic mysticism. He believed that people could attain identification with the Divine spirit through intense concentration.

Ma'aseh Bereshit: Literally "the act of creation," it refers to a specific school of mystical thought that speculates about the creation of the world.

Ma'aseh Merkabah: Literally "word of the chariot," it is also called *merkabah* mysticism. It refers to apocalyptic visions and a mystical perception of the throne of God in its chariot, as described in the first chapter of the Book of Ezekiel.

Maimonides, Moses (1135–1204): Moses ben Maimon, also called the RaMBaM, one of the great philosophers in all of Jewish history. Under the influence of Aristotelian thought, he was perhaps best known for his *Guide for the Perplexed* and his compilation of Jewish law in his volume *Mishnah Torah*.

Makor Chayim: Literally "the source of life," it refers to the name of several works of literature, including a philosophic treatise by the philosopher and poet Solomon ibn Gabirol.

Malchut: Literally "kingdom," the tenth level of the *sefirot* in kabbalah.

Mendelssohn, Moses (1729–1786): Philosopher par excellence of the German Enlightenment who worked in the struggle for civil rights for the Jews. He was the first to translate the Bible into German.

Monotheism: Belief in one supreme God.

Musar: Ethical guidance and advice to encourage strict behavior regarding Jewish law. It developed into a full-scale literature in the nineteenth century.

Nachmanides (1194–1270): Moses ben Nachman or the RaMBaN, a leading Spanish commentator in the Middle Ages. Most of his work focused on the Talmud and Halacha.

Negative Attributes, Doctrine of: As articulated by Moses Maimonides, once one begins to try to list the attributes of God, knowing full well that the list must be concluded without fully expressing all the attributes, we therefore limit God. As a result, we should not try to list any attributes.

Neo-Orthodoxy: Originated as a modern faction of German Orthodoxy, originally used in a derogatory sense. Essentially connected to Samson Raphael Hirsch.

Neoplatonism: Platonism modified in later antiquity to accord with Aristotelian, post-Aristotelian, and oriental conceptions. It conceives of the world as an emanation from the One with whom the soul is capable of being reunited in trance or ecstasy.

Nous: A philosophic term for reason.

Ontology: The branch of metaphysics concerned with discovering the true nature of reality and its laws.

Pantheism: Philosophy that equates God with the forces and laws of the universe.

Particularism: A focus on Israel's unique relationship with God rather than God's general relationship with the world.

Peoplehood: A variant construct of the philosophy of Mordecai Kaplan in describing Judaism as a peoplehood rather than a religion.

Philo (Judaeus) of Alexandria (ca. 20 B.C.E.–50 C.E.): Philosopher whose Greek writings primarily focused on the Torah.

Plaskow, Judith: Feminist theologian, best known for her 1979 landmark book on feminist spirituality *Womanspirit Rising*.

Progressive Judaism: A synonym for Reform Judaism.

Radical Amazement: Phrase coined by Abraham Joshua Heschel, it refers to individual experiences of the divine in this world. Heschel argues for an extraordinary sensitivity to the hidden reality inherent in the seemingly ordinary.

Rational Commandments: According to Saadia Gaon, commandments that have their basis in reason.

Rationalism: Reliance on reason as the basis for the establishment of religious truth.

Reconstructionist Judaism: The institutionalized movement whose foundation emanated from the philosophy of Mordecai Kaplan, its founder. It argues that Jewish beliefs have broken down, and Jewish identity, therefore, needs to be nurtured so that the Jewish historical belief in salvation in the world to come can be transformed into a belief in salvation in this world. Kaplan further defined Judaism as an evolving civilization whose common denominator is the continuous life of the Jewish people.

Redemption: Generally refers to deliverance by God. In philosophy, it refers to a sign that God triumphed over evil.

Reform Judaism: The first modern movement to develop as a result of changes in Europe brought about as a result of emancipation.

Reines, Alvin (1926–): Twentieth-century philosopher who argues that Reform Judaism is a "polydoxy" (i.e., combination of several approaches). Rejecting divine revelation and mitzvah, he has transformed Bar Mitzvah, the son of the commandment, into Baal Mitzvah, the master of the commandment.

Religion of Reason: Moses Mendelssohn's belief that Judaism is a universal religion of reason. Eternal truths, which are self-evident to reason, are opposed to temporal truths, which are subject to experiences of sensation. Hermann Cohen also uses this term in a similar fashion.

Religious Consciousness: According to Leo Baeck, the individual must move beyond assigning only ethical monotheism to Judaism. For Baeck, rationalism alone could not adequately explain Judaism. Thus, consciousness points to a realm beyond the scientific-ethical rationalism. Baeck therefore speaks to the consciousness of mystery as the deepest root of our religiosity.

Religious Empiricism: Knowledge of the existence and

nature of God as originating through a person's sense experience.

Revelation: The act of communication from God to humans and the content of such communication. Often specifically refers to the experience at Mount Sinai when God gave the Torah to the Jewish people through Moses.

Reward and Punishment: A concept from rabbinic Judaism that suggests that God rewards good acts and punishes those who do evil—to take place in the world to come.

Rosenzweig, Franz (1886–1929): Philosopher and theologian whose major work was *The Star of Redemption*. An exponent of existentialism, he rejected the notion of traditional philosophy that the three elements we encounter in experience—God, man, and the world—all share the same essence. He argued that they are separate entities with independent existence.

Rubenstein, Richard (1924–): Theologian primarily associated with the post-Holocaust "God is Dead" movement. He argues that we should reject the notion of a chosen people since the Holocaust means that we are the suffering servant.

Saadia Gaon (882–942): He is considered the father of medieval Jewish philosophy. Most of his works are colored by a polemic against Karaism. His major work combines an exposition of his own thinking with a criticism of opposing viewpoints.

Schechter, Solomon (1847–1925): Scholar and president of the Jewish Theological Seminary of America. He was considered to be the chief architect of Conservative Judaism.

Schneersohn, Menachem (1902–1995): The most recent Lubavitcher Rebbe, he continued to build the Chabad community worldwide.

Sefer HaIkkarim: The book of basic ideas, prepared by Joseph Albo. It is devoted to a discussion of Jewish dogmas.

Sefirot: A fundamental aspect of kabbalah, a term coined by the author of *Sefer Yetzirah*. It denotes the ten stages that emanate from the Ein Sof (God) and from God's manifestation in each of God's ten attributes.

Soloveitchik, Joseph (1902–1993): Orthodox rabbi and foremost proponent of modern orthodoxy, the fusion of classic Halakhic Judaism and American culture, epitomized by graduates of Yeshiva University. His many published papers focus on the human condition—what it means to be an individual in relation to God in the context of Jewish tradition.

Spinoza, Baruch (1632–1677): Dutch philosopher excommunicated from the Jewish community because his thinking was not in accord with Jewish thought. Best considered a pantheist, he advanced a polemic point of view against the Bible.

Star of Redemption: The primary work of Franz Rosenzweig, divided into the classic section of creation, revelation, and redemption, in which he seeks to demonstrate what existence says about God, the world, and the human species, as well as how the relationships are drawn among them.

Steinberg, Milton (1903–1950): Conservative rabbi and philosopher who concerned himself with a philosophic approach to Judaism.

Steinheim, Solomon (1789–1866): Philosopher whose work *Revelation According to the Doctrine of the Synagogue* was opposed to all philosophic rationalism. In its stead, he developed a doctrine that stated that the religious truth was given exclusively in revelation.

Teleology: The study of the evidences of the design of nature.

Theology: The study of God.

Theophany: Referring to any visible manifestation of a deity.

Tikkun: Literally "repair." According to the kabbalists, it is essential to bring about world order by repairing the vessels that were broken by God at creation.

Transcendence and Immanence of God: Philosophic concepts that describe the paradoxical concept of a Supreme Being who can be both "close" to humankind as well as "distant" from humankind.

Transubstantiation: The change in the Eucharistic elements at their consecration in the Mass from the substance of bread and wine to the substance of the body and blood of Jesus.

Trinity: The unity of Father, Son, and Holy Spirit as three persons in one godhead.

Universalism: In opposition to particularism, this refers to a Jewish posture that rejects the election of Israel as a chosen people. Instead, it seems the mission of Israel as a light unto the nations.

When Bad Things Happen to Good People: A best-selling book by Rabbi Harold Kushner that basically describes a limited God who does not directly impact on what happens to people in the world.

Wissenschaft des Judenthums: Literally "the science of Judaism," this term refers to the scientific, critical study of Judaism using modern methods of research, historically allied with German Reform Judaism.

Zunz, Leopold (1794–1886): Among the founders of Wissenschaft des Judenthums in Germany, his chief interest was research in Hebrew liturgy.

FURTHER READING

Agus, J. B. (1941). *Modern Philosophies of Judaism: A Study of Recent Jewish Philosophies of Religion*. New York: Behrman House.

Bergman, S. (1960). *In His Image: The Jewish Philosophy of Man as Expressed in Rabbinic Tradition*. London and New York: Abelard-Schuman.

Berkovits, E. (1959). *God, Man and History*. New York: Jonathan David.

——— (1973). *Faith After the Holocaust*. New York: Ktav.

Borowitz, E. (1968). *A New Jewish Theology in the Making*. Philadelphia: Westminster.

Cohen, A. A. ed. (1970). *Arguments and Doctrines: A Reader of Jewish Thinking in the Aftermath of the Holocaust*. Philadelphia: Jewish Publication Society and New York: Harper and Row.

Cohon, S. S. (1971). *Jewish Theology*. New York: Humanities.

Dorff, E. N. (1977). *Conservative Judaism: Our Ancestors to Our Descendants*. New York: United Synagogue Youth.

Efron B. ed. (1965). *Currents and Trends in Contemporary Jewish Thought*. New York: Ktav.

Eisenstein, I. (1953). *Creative Judaism*. New York: Jewish Reconstructionist Foundation.

Emet Ve-Emunah: *Statement of Principles of Conservative Judaism*. (1988). Jewish Theological Seminary of America, by the Rabbinical Assembly and the United Synagogue of America.

Guttman, J. (1988). *The Philosophy of Judaism*, trans. D. W. Silverman. New Jersey: Jason Aronson.

Herberg, W. (1951). *Judaism and Modern Man: An Interpretation of Jewish Religion*. New York: Farrar, Straus and Cudahy.

Heschel, A. J. (1965). *Between God and Man: An Interpretation of Judaism from the Writings of Abraham J. Heschel*, F. A. Rothschild. New York: Harper and Bros.

Maybaum, I. (1965). *The Face of God after Auschwitz*. Amsterdam: Polak and Van Gennep.

Neusner, J. ed. (1973). *Understanding Jewish Theology*. New York: Ktav.

Rubenstein, R. L. (1966). *After Auschwitz*. Indianapolis: Bobbs-Merrill.

Schechter, S. (1909). *Aspects of Rabbinic Theology*. New York: Schocken Books.

Silverman, W. (1970). *Basic Reform Judaism*. New York: Philosophical Library.

Soloveitchik, J. B. (1965). *The Lonely Man of Faith*. Tradition, vol. 7, no. 2.

Steinberg, M. (1960). *Anatomy of Faith*, ed. A. Cohen. New York: Harcourt Brace.

Weinstein, J. (1970). *Maimonides the Educator*. New York: Pedagogic Library.

——— (1975). *Buber and Humanistic Education*. New York: Philosophical Library.

INDEX

Aaron ben Meir, 21
Abrabanel, Isaac
  Biblical commentaries of,
    84–85
  exegetic innovations of,
    88–89
  on history, 87–88
  life and works of, 83–84
  Messianic thought of, 86–87,
    88
  religious philosophy of,
    85–86
Abraham ibn Ezra, 37, 114, 115
Action, Abraham Heschel on,
    201
Active intellect, 19, 71
Adam
  dualistic interpretation of,
    189–190
  Isaac Luria on, 96

Adult education, 154
Adultery, 144
Agudat Israel, 122
Ahavat yisrael (love for fellow
    Jews), 182–183
Albo, Joseph, 79–82
Alkabiz, Solomon, 93
Allegory
  Aristobulus and, 8
  Isaac Abrabanel on, 85
  Philo Judaeus and, 9
Almohades, 47
Anti-Semitism, 212
Arabic, 17, 22
Arama, Isaac, 84
Aristobulus of Paneas, 8
Aristotelianism, 19–20
  Hasdai Crescas and, 74–75,
    76
  Ibn Daud and, 44, 46

Aristotelianism (*continued*)
  Isaac Abrabanel and, 88
  Levi ben Gershom and, 72
Aristotle
  on divine providence, 70
  on God's knowledge, 69
As a Driven Leaf (Steinberg),
  177–178
Ashkenazic Jews, 226
Atheism, 104–105
Attributes, of God
  humanistic view of, 195–196
  negative, 11, 18–19
  positive, 69, 76–77
Augustine, Saint, 84
Auschwitz. *See* Holocaust
Authoritarian religion, 194
Avicenna. *See* Ibn Sina
Awareness, of God, 200–202
Azariah dei Ross, 15

Baal Shem Tov, 203
Baal teshuvah movement, 185
Babylonian Judaism, 21
Bachya ibn Pakuda, 26, 33–36
Baeck, R. Leo, 149–152
Bar Mitzvah, 211
Bat Kol (Divine Voice), 86
Becoming, concept of Being
  and, 137–138
Being
  concept of becoming and,
  137–138
  God as, 11
Belzer, Isaac, 130

Berkovits, R. Eliezer, 213–216
Bernays, R. Isaac, 117
Bible. *See also* Pentateuch
  history and, 87
  passages cited by Jewish
    philosophers, 2–4
Biblical criticism
  of Aristobulus, 8
  of Isaac Abrabanel, 83–85
  of Levi ben Gershom, 67–68
  of Nachmonides, 62–63
  of Philo Judaeus, 9–10
  of Rosenzweig, 154–155
  of Spinoza, 104
Biblical translation
  by Rosenzweig and Buber,
    154
  by Samson Hirsch, 121
Binah (wisdom), 93, 96
Body
  evil and, 14
  in Greek philosophy, 11
  Menachem Schneersohn on,
    183
  Neo-platonism on, 19
  Saadia Gaon on, 25
  soul and, 29
  Spinoza on, 102
Bondage, 102–103
Book of Beliefs and Opinions
  (Saadia Gaon), 22, 23
Book of Mystic Splendor, 92
Book of Principles (Joseph
  Albo), 79–81

Book of Tradition (Ibn Daud), 43, 46
Borowitz, Eugene, 232
Breaking of the vessels, 94–95
Bruno, Giordano, 77
Buber, Martin, 121, 139
  Abraham Heschel and, 197
  on evil, 168
  existential philosophy and, 163
  Franz Rosenzweig and, 153, 154, 156
  Hasidut movement and, 160–162
  Haskalah movement and, 162
  humanistic education and, 168–170
  influences on, 159–160
  "I–Thou" relationship of, 164–167
  life of, 160

Capitalism, 146
Catholic Israel, 141, 142–143
Causes, 19
Centenary Perspective, of Reform Judaism, 231, 232–233
Ceremonial laws, 25
Charity, 183
Chavurah movement, 172
Chavurot, 172, 176
Chaya, 96
Chayim, R. Joseph, 83

Chmielnicki, Bodgen, 160
Chochmah (wisdom), 93, 96
Chosenness. *See also* Jewish People
  Abraham Kook on, 147–148
  anti-Semitism and, 212
  Conservative Judaism and, 239
  Mordecai Kaplan on, 174–175
  Orthodox Judaism and, 229
Christiani, Pablo, 61
Christianity
  anti-Semitism and, 212
  "death of God" theology and, 210
  Franz Rosenzweig and, 156
  Hasdai Crescas and, 73–74
  Isaac Abrabanel and, 84, 87
  Joseph Albo and, 81, 82
  Judah Halevi and, 40–41
  Leo Baeck and, 152
  Moses Mendelssohn and, 111–112
  Philo Judaeus and, 15
  Solomon ibn Gabirol and, 31
Churban (destruction), 218
Civilization, Judaism as, 172–173, 244
Civil rights, 110–111
Cohen, Hermann, 135–139, 150, 151, 153, 193
Cohen, Morris Raphael, 177

Columbus Platform, of Reform Judaism, 231, 234, 235
Commandments. *See also Mitzvot*
  Bachya ibn Pakuda on, 35
  Franz Rosenzweig on, 156
  Hasdai Crescas on, 74
  Maimonides on, 53, 56
  Samson Hirsch on, 120–121
Communication, between God and humans, 12
Communion, 76
Community, 141, 142–143. *See also* Jewish people
  Abraham Heschel on, 201
  Conservative Judaism and, 239
  "covenantal," 188
  "death of God" theology and, 210–211
Community centers, 175
Conservative Judaism, 132, 133, 144
  Abraham Heschel and, 198
  Franz Rosenzweig and, 157
  God and, 237
  halachah and, 238–239
  history of, 235–237
  ideals of, 240–241
  the Jewish people and, 239
  modern Israel and, 239–240
  revelation and, 237–238
  social justice and, 240
Contemplation, 8

Contingency, in proof of God's existence, 44
Contraction, as stage of creation, 94
Conventional law, 82
Cordovero, Moses, 93
Corporeal existence, 24
Correlation, Hermann Cohen's concept of, 138, 139
Covenant, 167
"Covenantal community," 188
Creation
  free will and, 24
  Hasdai Crescas on, 76
  importance of number seven to, 8
  Isaac Luria on, 94–96
  Levi ben Gershom on, 70–71
  Nachmonides on, 62
  Philo Judaeus on, 13
  Saadia Gaon on, 23–24
Crescas, Hasdai, 72, 73–77, 79
Crown, as *sefirah*, 93, 96
Custom, 142, 243

Daniel, 87, 88
David ben Gurion, 104
"Death of God," 209–211
Deeds, Abraham Heschel on, 201
Derech eretz (modern culture), 119
Desire, 129, 144

Dessau, Moses. *See*
    Mendelssohn, R. Moses
Devekut (communion with
    God), 76
Dialogical philosophy, 159.
    See also "I–Thou"
    relationship
Dietary laws, 25
Disobedience, 143–144
Divine commandments. *See*
    Mitzvot
"Divine concern," 199, 200
Divine emanations. *See Sefirot*
Divine influence. *See Ha-Inyan
    ha-Elohi*
Divine law, 80, 81–82
"Divine pathos," 202
Divine Voice. *See Bat Kol*
Divine will, 29
Dogma, 111
Dorff, Elliot, 237
Dualism, in human nature,
    189–190
Duties of the Heart (Bachya
    ibn Pakuda), 33–35, 36
Duty, 139

Ecclesiastes, 114
Education. *See also* Jewish
    schools
    Franz Rosenzweig and, 154
    Israel Salanter and, 127
    Joseph Soloveitchik and,
        191
    Maimonides and, 57–59

Martin Buber and, 168–170
Menachem Schneersohn
    and, 184
Orthodox Judaism and,
    226–227
Samson Hirsch and, 119
Ein Sof (The Infinite One), 93
Eisenstein, R. Ira, 241
Emanation, 18
Emotion, in religion, 143
Enden, Van den, 99–100
Enlightenment
    Jewish, 162
    philosophy of, 108–109
Epicureans, 4
Epicurus, 4
"Epoch-making events," 218,
    223
Eschatology, 72. *See also*
    Messianism
Essence, of God, 10
Eternity, of God, 50
Ethical monotheism, 137, 151,
    232, 235
Ethics
    Bachya ibn Pakuda on,
        33–35
    Hermann Cohen on,
        136–137
    Israel Salanter on, 127,
        128–129
    Leo Baeck on, 151
    Solomon ibn Gabirol on,
        29–30
Ethics (Spinoza), 100, 101, 102

Ettlinger, R. Jacob, 117
Etymology, speculative, 120
Evil. See also Theodicy
  body and, 14
  evolutionary theory of,
    178–179
  explanations of, 205–207
  Isaac Luria on, 94, 95
  Leo Baeck on, 151–152
  Levi ben Gershom on, 70
  limited theism and, 180
  Maimonides on, 56
  Martin Buber on, 168
  Mordecai Kaplan on, 175
  Philo Judaeus on, 13–14
  "radical," 168
Evil inclination, 143–144
Evolutionary theory, of evil,
  178–179
Excommunication, of Spinoza,
  100, 104
Exegesis, Isaac Abrabanel and,
  88–89
Existence, God and, 24
Existence, of God
  faith and, 178
  as fundamental principle, 81
  Hasdai Crescas on, 75
  Levi ben Gershom on, 68
  Maimonides on, 54–55
  Moses Mendelssohn on, 109
  Philo Judaeus on, 10
Existentialism, 157
  applied to education,
    168–170

  Joseph Soloveitchik and,
    189–190
  Martin Buber and, 163

Fackenheim, R. Emil, 218, 219,
  221–224
Faith
  Bachya ibn Pakuda on, 34
  Maimonides' principles of,
    49–54
  Milton Steinberg on, 178
Fear, in communication with
  God, 12
Five Books of Moses. See
  Pentateuch
Folkways, 243
Form
  Solomon ibn Gabirol on,
    28–29
  theory of, 13
Fraenkel, R. David, 107
Frankel, R. Zechariah, 131–
  133, 235–236
Frankfurter, Mendel, 117
Freedom. See Free will;
  Religious freedom
Free will
  creation and, 24
  Hasdai Crescas on, 75–76
  "hiding of God's face" and,
    214–215, 216
  Ibn Daud on, 45
  Leo Baeck on, 152
  Levi ben Gershom on, 69
  Milton Steinberg on, 178

Moses Mendelssohn on, 110
Saadia Gaon on, 25–26
Spinoza on, 102–103
Fromm, Eric, 193–196

Gaon/geonim (genius), 21
Geiger, R. Abraham, 117, 118–
     119, 123–125
Genesis, 9–10
Geonic period, 21
Gersonides. *See* Levi ben
     Gershom
Gezerah (evil decree), 218
God
     becoming aware of,
          200–202
     as Being, 137
     communication with, 12
     communion with, 76
     Conservative Judaism and,
          237
     "death of," 209–211
     "divine concern" and, 199,
          200
     essence of, 10
     eternity of, 50
     evil and, 13–14, 207
     existence of, 10, 54–55, 68,
          74–75, 81, 109, 178
     as first principle, 18, 49
     free will and, 45
     Hermann Cohen on,
          136–137
     hiddenness of, 168,
          214–215, 216

in history, 215, 216, 222
humanistic view of,
     195–196
incorporeality of, 50
Isaac Abrabanel on, 87–88
"I–Thou" relationship and,
     167
justice of, 18
kabbalah and, 93–94
logos and, 13
love and, 76
in Luria's stages of creation,
     94–96
name of, 11
naturalistic concept of,
     173–174
negative attributes and, 11,
     18–19
negative theology and,
     55–56
omniscience of, 52–53,
     69–70
Orthodox Judaism and, 228
paradox about, 150
positive attributes and, 69,
     76–77
as Prime Mover, 44, 55
providence of, 70
Reconstructionist Judaism
     and, 242
Reform Judaism and,
     223–233
relationship with humankind,
     138, 155–156, 190, 202
Saadia Gaon on, 24

God (*continued*)
Spinoza on, 101
trust in, 35–36
uniqueness of, 44–45, 55–56
unity of, 11, 18, 44–45, 49–50, 54–55
Godliness, 173–174
God's Presence in History (Berkovits), 214
Goodness, natural, 14, 15
Greek philosophy, 11. *See also* Hellenism
Guide for the Perplexed (Maimonides), 48–49

Ha-Ari. *See* Luria, R. Isaac
Ha-Inyan ha-Elohi (divine influence), 41
Halachah
Conservative Judaism and, 238–239
Holocaust and, 219
Joseph Soloveitchik and, 188–189, 191
Levi ben Gershom and, 68
Nachmonides and, 63–64
Reconstructionist Judaism and, 242
Saadia Gaon and, 22, 26
Zechariah Frankel and, 132–133
Halevi, Judah, 37–42
Happiness. *See also* Joy
Abraham Heschel on, 200
Joseph Albo on, 80, 81–82

Maimonides on, 56
Saadia Gaon on, 25
Hasidism. *See also* Hasidut movement
Abraham Heschel and, 203
Menachem Schneersohn and, 181–185
Hasidut movement, 160–162
Haskalah movement, 112, 162
Hebrew, 17
Samson Hirsch on, 118
Samuel Luzzatto on, 115
Hebrew Union College, 230
Hellenism, 7–8. *See also* Greek philosophy
Hertzberg, Arthur, 100
Heschel, Abraham Joshua
on becoming aware of God, 200–202
on being human, 200
influence of, 202–203
life of, 197–198, 199
on medieval Jewish philosophy, 202
religious philosophy of, 198–199
Hester panim (hiding of God's face), 168, 214–215, 216
"Hiding of God's face," 168, 214–215, 216
Hirsch, R. Samson Raphael
Abraham Geiger and, 117, 118–119, 123
biblical translations of, 121

on commandments,
120–121
conception of Judaism,
119–120
on education, 119
on Jewish people, 121–122
life of, 117–118
Orthodox movement and,
117, 118, 119, 122
Reform movement and,
118–119
History
Abraham Kook on, 148
Emil Fackenheim on, 218,
222–224
God and, 215, 216, 222
Ignaz Maybaum on, 218
Isaac Abrabanel on, 87–88
Judah Halevi on, 41
Reform Judaism on, 232
Hitler, Adolf
Emil Fackenheim on, 224
as God's agent, 219
Holiness, 188–189
Holocaust
"death of God" theology
and, 209–211
as devoid of explanation,
222
Emil Fackenheim on,
221–224
as "epoch-making event,"
218–219, 223
"hiding of God's face" and,
168, 214–215, 216

Menachem Schneersohn on,
183
problem of evil and, 205
"radical evil" and, 168
Reform Judaism on,
217–219
Holy spirit, 138
Horowitz, R. Joseph, 130
Humanism
Eric Fromm and, 193–196
Mordecai Kaplan and, 242
Moses Mendelssohn and,
112
Humanistic education,
168–170
Humanistic religion, 194
Humanity, Abraham Heschel
on, 200
Humankind
communication with God,
12
holiness and, 188–189
"I–Thou" relationship and,
166–167
love for God, 76
relationship with God, 138,
155–156, 190, 202
Human nature
dualism and, 189–190
Saadia Gaon on, 25–26
Humility, 34

Ibn Daud, Abraham ben David
Halevi, 43–46
Ibn Sina, 44, 45, 46

Idolatry, 144
"I–It" relationship, 164, 165–166, 168
Ikkarim (principles), 80–81
"Imitation of God," 195
Immortality
  Levi ben Gershom on, 70
  Moses Mendelssohn on, 109–110
Incorporeality, of God, 50
Intellect
  active, 19, 71
  Joseph Albo on, 80, 82
  Solomon ibn Gabirol on, 29
Intellectualism, secular, 163
Intellectual love, 101, 103
Intermediaries, in communication with God, 12
Isaiah, 114
Islam, 17, 40–41
Israel. *See also* Jewish people
  Abraham Kook on, 147–148
  community of, 141, 142–143
  God and, 15
  Judah Halevi on, 41
  Samson Hirsch on, 121
Israel, Land of
  Abraham Kook on, 146, 147–148
  Isaac Abrabanel on, 88
  Orthodox Judaism and, 229
  Reconstructionist Judaism and, 243–244
  Samson Hirsch on, 121

Israel, State of
  Abraham Heschel on, 199
  Conservative Judaism and, 239–240
  Eliezer Berkovits on, 215
  Emil Fackenheim on, 224
  Menachem Schneersohn on, 184
  Orthodox Judaism and, 229
  Reconstructionist Judaism and, 243–244
  Reform Judaism and, 234
  Richard Rubenstein on, 211, 212
"I–Thou" relationship, 164–167
  applied to education, 168–170

Jerome, Saint, 84, 89
Jewish-Christian debates, 61
Jewish community centers, 175
Jewish Enlightenment, 162
Jewish Free University, 154
Jewish law. *See* Halachah; Law
Jewish nationality, Abraham Kook on, 147–148
Jewish people. *See also* Chosenness; Community; Israel
  Conservative Judaism and, 239
  Orthodox Judaism and, 229
  Reconstructionist Judaism and, 243

Reform Judaism and,
  234–235
Jewish philosophy
  concerns of, 1
  Enlightenment rationalism
    and, 108–109
  frequent biblical verses in,
    2–4
  history of, 1–2
  medieval period, 17–20,
    202
  modern, 99–100
  origins of, 7–8
  rabbinic literature and, 4–5
Jewish religion. *See* Judaism
Jewish schools, 144, 185, 188
Jewish Theological Seminary,
  142, 236
Job, 63
Joy, 143. *See also* Happiness
Jubilee year, 146–147
Judaism. *See also* individual
    denominations
  Babylonian, 21
  as civilization, 172–173, 244
  "death of God" theology
    and, 210–211
  denominations in America,
    225–226
  Eric Fromm on, 195, 196
  institutions of, 225
  Leo Baeck on, 151
  Milton Steinberg on,
    179–180

Moses Mendelssohn on, 111
psychoanalytic interpreta-
    tion of, 211–212
Samson Hirsch on, 119–120
Judaism As A Civilization
  (Kaplan), 172–173
Justice, of God, 18

Kabbalah, 91–92
  on God, 93–94
  Hasdai Crescas and, 77
  Isaac Abrabanel and, 85
  Luria's five souls and, 96–97
  Luria's three stages of
    creation in, 94–96
Kant, Immanuel, 135, 138–139
Kaplan, R. Mordecai, 171–176,
    177, 241, 242, 243, 244
Karo, Joseph, 93
Kelippot (shells), 95, 96
Keter (crown), 93, 96
Kiddush HaShem, 214
Kierkegaard, Søren, 163
Kimchi, David, 85
King, Martin Luther, Jr., 198
Kingdom, as *sefirah*, 93, 96
Kingdom of God, 156
Kisch, Abraham, 107
Klaal Yisrael (community of
    Israel), 142, 239
Knowledge
  human and divine, 69–70
  Moses Mendelssohn on, 108
  Saadia Gaon on, 23

Knowledge (*continued*)
  scientific, Hermann Cohen on, 136
  Spinoza on, 102
Kook, R. Abraham Isaac, 145–148
Koran, 125
Krause, Ludwig, 193
Kushner, R. Harold, 180
The Kuzari (Judah Halevi), 38–40, 42

Land of Israel. *See* Israel, Land of
Law. *See also* Halachah; *Mitzvot*
  categories of, 25, 82
  community of Israel and, 142–143
  Hermann Cohen on, 139
  Joseph Albo on, 80, 81–82
  natural, 82, 101
  Oral, 63
  Philo Judaeus and, 9
  revelation and, 111, 156
  Samson Hirsch on, 120
Learning, Abraham Heschel on, 201. *See also* Education
Lessing, G.E., 107
Levi ben Gershom, R., 67–72, 84
Light of God (Hasdai Crescas), 74–76, 77
Limited theism, 178, 180
Liturgical poems, 26, 42

Liturgy
  Saadia Gaon and, 26
  Solomon ibn Gabirol and, 30, 31
Logic, Aristotelian, 19, 20
Logos, 13
Loneliness, 189–190
Love
  as *ahavat yisrael*, 182–183
  in communication with God, 12
  between God and humans, 76
  intellectual, 101, 103
Lubavitch Hasidism, 181–185
Luria, R. Isaac
  five souls of, 96–97
  on God, 93–94
  life of, 92–93
  three stages of creation and, 94–96
Luzzatto, Samuel David, 113–116

Mahdi ibn Tumart, 47
Maimonides, Moses
  Abraham Heschel on, 202
  on creation, 70–71
  on divine commandments, 56
  educational philosophy of, 57–59
  on evil, 56
  on God's existence, 54–55
  on God's knowledge, 69

Hasdai Crescas on, 75, 76
influence of, 59–60
Isaac Abrabanel on, 85–86
life and works of, 47–49
naturalism and, 87
negative theology of, 55–56
principles of faith, 49–54
Samuel Luzzatto and, 114, 115

Malchut (kingdom), 93, 96
Martyrdom, 214
Marxism, Spinoza and, 105
Maskilim, 162
Matter, Solomon ibn Gabirol on, 28, 29
Maybaum, R. Ignaz, 217–219
Medicine, Joseph Albo and, 79
Mekor Chayim (Solomon ibn Gabirol), 28, 31
Mendelssohn, R. Moses
Christianity and, 111–112
civil rights and, 110–111
Haskalah movement and, 112
on Judaism, 111
life of, 107–108
religious philosophy of, 108–110
Menorah, 184–185
Messiah
Hasdai Crescas on, 77
Isaac Abrabanel on, 86–87, 88
Isaac Luria on, 96, 97
Joseph Albo on, 81

Levi ben Gershom on, 72
Maimonides on, 53
Solomon Schechter on, 144
Messianism
Hermann Cohen on, 138
Isaac Abrabanel and, 88
Martin Buber on, 167
natural life and, 211
Zechariah Frankel and, 132
Metaphysical theory, of evil, 206
Milchamot Adonai (Levi ben Gershom), 68–72
Mind
God as, 178
morality and, 14
Spinoza on, 102
universal, 10, 11
Miracles
Levi ben Gershom on, 71–72
Mordecai Kaplan on, 175
Reform Judaism on, 232
Spinoza on, 101
"Mission" theory, 234–235, 243
Mitzvot
Hermann Cohen on, 139
Isaac Luria on, 95
Maimonides on, 56
Mordecai Kaplan on, 174–175
Nachmonides on, 63
Orthodox Judaism and, 228–229

Mitzvot (*continued*)
  Reconstructionist Judaism
    and, 242–243
  Reform Judaism and, 233–
    234, 235
  Saadia Gaon on, 25
  Samuel Luzzatto on, 115
Monotheism, ethical, 232, 235
Morais, R. Sabato, 236
Morality
  Aristotelianism on, 19
  free will and, 215
  Kant's doctrine of, 139
  Maimonides on, 56
  Mordecai Kaplan on, 174
  Philo Judaeus on, 14–15
  piety and, 147
Moral theory, of evil, 205–206
Moses
  Joseph Albo on, 81
  Maimonides on, 51–52
  Spinoza on, 101
Moses ben Maimon. *See*
  Maimonides, Moses
Moses ben Menachem-Mendel.
  See Mendelssohn, R. Moses
Moses ben Nachman. *See*
  Nachmonides
Moses ibn Ezra, 26, 37
Musar (moral instruction), 127,
  128
Musar movement, 127, 128,
  129–130
Mutazilite Kalam, 18

"Mystery," dialectic with
  "command," 150–151
Mysticism, 146, 198. *See also*
  Kabbalah

Nachmonides, 61–65
Nationality, Jewish, 147–148
Natural goodness, 14, 15
Naturalism
  Isaac Abrabanel and, 87–88
  Mordecai Kaplan and, 173–
    174, 242
Natural law, 82, 101
Nature
  "I–Thou" relationship and,
    166
  return to, 211
  Solomon ibn Gabirol on, 29
  as source of evil, 178–179
Necessity, in proof of God's
  existence, 44
Nefesh, 96
Negative attributes, in
  describing God, 11,
  18–19
Negative theology, 55–56
Neo-Aristotelianism, 48–49,
  59
Neo-Kantianism, 135
Neo-Orthodoxy, 117–122
Neo-Platonism, 18–19, 28
Neshamah, 96
Nissim ben Reuben, R., 73
Nobel, Nehemiah, 193

Nous (mind), 14
Novellas, of Nachmonides, 63, 65

Oenomaus of Gadara, 4
Omniscience, of God, 52–53, 69–70
Oneness. *See* Unity
Ontology, in proof of God's existence, 109
Ontos (being), 11
Or Adonai (Hasdai Crescas), 74–76, 77
Oral Law, 63
Orthodox Judaism
  in America, 226–227
  God and, 228
  the Jewish people and, 229
  Joseph Soloveitchik and, 187–191
  modern Israel and, 229
  revelation and, 228
  Samson Hirsch and, 117–122
  Torah and, 228–229

Palestine, 152. *See also* Israel, Land of; Israel, State of
Pantheism, 101
Passion
  evil and, 144
  Israel Salanter on, 129
Pentateuch
  Aristobulus on, 8
  Philo Judaeus on, 9–10

Samuel Luzzatto and, 113, 114
Spinoza on, 104
Personal freedom. *See* Free will
Phaedon (Mendelssohn), 108, 109
Philo Judaeus, 7, 9–15
Philo of Alexandria. *See* Philo Judaeus
Philosophic etymology, 120
Philosophic socialism, 138
Philosophy. *See also* Jewish philosophy
  critical reaction to, 19–20
  Hermann Cohen on, 135–136
  Torah and, 44
Piety
  Leo Baeck on, 151
  morality and, 147
Pines, Shlomo, 60
Piyyutim (liturgical poems), 26, 42
Plato, 13
Poetry
  Judah Halevi and, 37, 41–42
  Solomon ibn Gabirol and, 30, 31
Poland, Hasidut movement and, 160–161
Political theory, of Spinoza, 103
Positive attributes, in describing God, 69, 76–77

"Positive-historical" school, 132, 236
Practice, in ethical development, 14, 15
Prayer
  Abraham Geiger on, 125
  Abraham Heschel on, 201
  Isaac Luria on, 95
  Maimonides on, 50–51
  Milton Steinberg on, 179
  Mordecai Kaplan on, 175
  Saadia Gaon and, 26
  Solomon ibn Gabirol and, 30
Prime Mover, 44, 55
Principles, Joseph Albo and, 80–81
Progressive Judaism, Leo Baeck and, 149–152
Propaedeutics, 84
Prophecy
  Abraham Geiger on, 124
  Hasdai Crescas on, 75
  Ibn Daud on, 45
  Isaac Abrabanel on, 86
  Judah Halevi on, 40
  reason and, 23
  Spinoza on, 101
Prophets
  Abraham Heschel on, 198–199
  Hermann Cohen on, 137
  Joseph Albo on, 81
  Maimonides on, 51

Providence, 70, 75
Psychoanalysis, interpretation of Judaism, 211–212
Punishment, divine, 110

Rabbinical Council of America, 227
Rabbinic literature
  Nachmonides and, 64–65
  Saadia Gaon and, 22, 26
  used in Jewish philosophy, 4–5
Rabbinic training, Zechariah Frankel and, 133
"Radical evil," 168
RaLBaG. See Levi ben Gershom
RaMBaM. See Maimonides, Moses
RaMBaN. See Nachmonides
RaMBeMaN. See Mendelssohn, R. Moses
RaN. See Nissim ben Reuben
Rashi. See Shlomo ben Isaac, R.
Rational commandments, 35
Rationalism
  Isaac Abrabanel on, 85
  Maimonides and, 48–49
  Moses Mendelssohn and, 108–109, 112
  Spinoza and, 103, 104
Rational law, 25
Reason
  Abraham Heschel on, 198
  Eric Fromm on, 194

Joseph Soloveitchik on, 188, 189
Moses Mendelssohn on, 108–109
rational law and, 25
revelation and, 23
Spinoza on, 101
Rebellion, sin as, 143–144
Reconstructionist Judaism, 176
in America, 244
God and, 242
history of, 172, 241
the Jewish people and, 243
on Judaism as civilization, 172–173
Land of Israel and, 243–244
naturalism and, 173–174
seal of, 241–242
social action and, 244
theological implications of, 174–175
Torah and, 242–243
Reform Judaism
Abraham Geiger and, 124–125
classical and modern approaches of, 235
Franz Rosenzweig and, 157
God and, 223–233
history of, 229–232
on Holocaust, 217–219
the Jewish people and, 234–235
mitzvot and, 233–234, 235
moderate, 132

Samson Hirsch and, 118–119
Torah and, 233
Relationships
between God and humankind, 138, 155–156, 190, 202
"I–Thou," 164–167
Reliable tradition, 23
Religion
Eric Fromm on, 194
twentieth-century issues in, 147
Religious consciousness, 151
Religious experience, 40
Religious freedom, 184–185
Religious pluralism, 240
Religious Zionism, 115
Repair of the world, 95–96, 97
Repentance, 152
Resurrection
Levi ben Gershom on, 72
Maimonides on, 53–54
Revealed religion
Moses Mendelssohn on, 111
Samson Hirsch on, 119–120
Revelation
Conservative Judaism and, 237–238
Franz Rosenzweig on, 155–156
as fundamental principle, 81
Holocaust and, 222, 223
Joseph Albo on, 82
kabbalah and, 91

Revelation (*continued*)
  law and, 25
  Martin Buber on, 167
  Moses Mendelssohn on, 111
  Orthodox Judaism and, 228
  reason and, 23
  Reform Judaism and, 233
  Samson Hirsch on, 119–120
Righteous, suffering and,
      13–14
Ritual, 211
Ritual law, 25
Ronsburg, Bazalel, 131
"Root experiences," 218, 223
Root principles, 80, 81
Rosenzweig, Franz, 139, 153–
      157, 217
Ruach, 96
Rubenstein, R. Richard, 209–212

Saadia Gaon
  halakhic works, 22, 26
  life of, 21–22
  liturgical works, 26
  philosophy of, 23–26
Sabbath
  kabbalism and, 97
  Nachmonides on, 62
Sacredness, 188–189
Salanter, R. Israel, 127–130
Salvation
  Isaac Abrabanel on, 88
  Mordecai Kaplan on, 174
  wisdom as, 101, 103
Samuel ben Meir, 114

Schechter, R. Solomon, 141–
      144, 171, 236
Schneersohn, R. Menachem
      Mendel, 181–185
Schools. *See* Jewish schools
Science
  God and, 173
  Hermann Cohen on, 136
Secular intellectualism, 163
Sefer Emunot ve-Deiot (Saadia
      Gaon), 22, 23
Sefer HaIkkarim (Joseph
      Albo), 79–81
Sefer HaKabbalah (Ibn Daud),
      43, 46
Sefirot (Divine emanations),
      93, 96, 97
Self-realization
  Eric Fromm and, 194
  evil and, 175
  Mordecai Kaplan on, 174
Separation of church and
      state, 184–185
Sephardic Jews, 226
Seven (number), creation
      and, 8
SHaDaL. *See* Luzzatto, Samuel
      David
Shells, 95, 96
Shevirat HaKelim (breaking of
      the vessels), 94–95
Shlomo ben Isaac, R., 114
Shorashim (root principles),
      80, 81
Shulchan Aruch, 229

Simcha shel mitzvah (joy of the law), 143
Sin, as rebellion, 143–144
Social action
    Reconstructionist Judaism and, 244
    Reform Judaism and, 235
Social ills, Milton Steinberg on, 179
Socialism, philosophic, 138
Social justice, Conservative Judaism and, 240
Social philosophy, Abraham Kook and, 146–147
Society for the Advancement of Judaism, 171, 172
Socratic method, 58
Solomon ibn Gabirol, 27–31
Solomon Schechter schools, 144
Soloveitchik, R. Joseph, 187–191, 229
Soul
    Aristotelianism on, 19
    Bachya ibn Pakuda on, 35
    body and, 29
    in Greek philosophy, 11
    Hasdai Crescas on, 77
    Ibn Daud on, 45
    Levi ben Gershom on, 70
    Menachem Schneersohn on, 183
    Moses Mendelssohn on, 109–110
    Neo-platonism on, 19

Saadia Gaon on, 25
Solomon ibn Gabirol on, 29
The Source of Life (Solomon ibn Gabirol), 28, 31
Spain, Almohades in, 47
Speculative etymology, 120
Spinoza, Baruch
    atheism and, 104–105
    biblical commentaries of, 104
    on body and mind, 102
    on freedom, 102–103
    on God's nature, 101
    Hasdai Crescas and, 77
    on knowledge, 102
    Levi ben Gershom and, 72
    life of, 99–100
    philosophy of, 100–101
    political theory of, 103
Star of Redemption (Rosenzweig), 154, 155–156
Steinberg, Milton, 177–180
Der Stern der Erloesung (Rosenzweig), 154, 155–156
Student-teacher relationship, 169. *See also* Education
Substance, Spinoza's theory of, 101
Suffering. *See also* Theodicy
    Eliezer Berkovits on, 214–215
    Ignaz Maybaum on, 217–219

Suffering (*continued*)
  of Israel, 41
  Philo Judaeus on, 13–14
Survival, as sacred obligation,
  223–224
Symbolism
  applied to commandments,
    120
  God and, 195
Syriac, 114

Talmud
  Nachmonides and, 63, 64
  Reform Judaism and, 233
  Zechariah Frankel on,
    132–133
Teachers. *See also* Education
  Maimonides on, 57
  Martin Buber on, 169
Teaching. *See also* Education
  in ethical development,
    14–15
  Maimonides on, 57–59
Teleology, Philo Judaeus and,
  10
Temple, destruction of, 218,
  223
Teshuvah (repentance), 152
Theism, limited, 178, 180
Theodicy, 26, 205–207
Theology
  "death of God" and,
    209–211
  of loneliness, 189–190
  negative, 55–56

pantheistic, 101
problem of evil and, 205–207
Theosophy, 91
Thomas Aquinas, 59, 81
Thought-Will, 178
Tikkun Middot HaNefesh
  (Solomon ibn Gabirol),
  27, 29–30
Tikkun (repair of the world),
  95–96, 97
Time, 14
Torah
  Conservative Judaism and,
    238
  Hasdai Crescas on, 75–76
  Judah Halevi on, 40
  Maimonides on, 51–52
  Nachmonides on, 62
  Orthodox Judaism and,
    228–229
  philosophy and, 44
  Reconstructionist Judaism
    and, 242–243
  Reform Judaism and, 233
  Samson Hirsch on, 119, 120
  Samuel Luzzatto on, 115
Tradition, reliable, 23
Traditional commandments,
  35
Traditional Judaism. *See*
  Orthodox Judaism
Trust, in God, 35–36
Truth, Franz Rosenzweig on,
  155
Tzimtzum (contraction), 94

Union of Orthodox Jewish Congregations, 227
Uniqueness, of God, 44–45, 55–56
United Synagogue of America, 142
United Synagogue of Conservative Judaism, 142
Unity
  Martin Buber on, 164
  Menachem Schneersohn on, 182–183
Unity, of God
  Ibn Daud on, 44–45
  Maimonides on, 49–50, 54–55
  Mutazilite Kalam on, 18
  Philo Judaeus on, 11
Universal Mind, 10, 11

Virtues, in worship of God, 35–36
Vital, Chayim, 93
Voice, Divine, 86

Wars of the Lord (Levi ben Gershom), 68–72
Weinstein, Joshua, 57, 58–59
Weiss, R. Isaac Mayer, 230
Wisdom
  as salvation, 101, 103
  as sefirah, 93, 96
Wise, R. Stephen S., 230

Women
  Maimonides on, 58
  Mordecai Kaplan and, 176
Working class, 136
World, Saadia Gaon's theory of, 23–24
World to Come, 53
World Union of Progressive Judaism, 149, 152
Worship
  Abraham Heschel on, 201
  Bachya ibn Pakuda on, 35–36
  Maimonides on, 50–51

Yechidah, 96
Yedidya. See Philo Judaeus
Yekutiel ben Isaac ibn Chasan, 27
Yeshiva University, 187, 188, 191, 227
Yetzer hara (evil inclination), 143–144

Zamosz, Israel, 107
Zionism
  Abraham Kook on, 146
  Eliezer Berkovits on, 215
  Hermann Cohen on, 139
  Leo Baeck on, 152
  Reform Judaism and, 234
  religious, 115
Zohar, 92

About the Author

Rabbi Ronald H. Isaacs is the spiritual leader of Temple Sholom in Bridgewater, New Jersey. He received his doctorate in instructional technology from Columbia University's Teacher's College. He is the author of numerous books, including *Loving Companions: Our Jewish Wedding Album*, co-authored with Leora Isaacs. Rabbi Isaacs currently serves on the editorial board of *Shofar* magazine and is a member of the Publications Committee of the Rabbinical Assembly. He resides in New Jersey with his wife, Leora, and their children, Keren and Zachary.